THE LIFE AND TIMES OF
JOHN WAYNE

HAMLYN

LONDON • NEW YORK • SYDNEY • TORONTO

Copyright ©1979 by Lorelei Publishing Company, Inc.
All rights reserved
Printed in U.S.A.
Published under arrangement with Ottenheimer Publishers, Inc.

First published in the U.K. 1979 by
The Hamlyn Publishing Group Limited
London • New York • Sydney • Toronto
Astronaut House, Feltham, Middlesex, England
ISBN: 0 600 39499 9

Three generations of moviegoers passed the time of life with John Wayne.

For half a century they sat in darkened theatres around the world and watched Wayne saddle up in more than two hundred films as he became the greatest figure in one of America's greatest native art forms, the Western.

They ranged from serials to four-reelers in which Wayne capitalized on the rage for singing cowboys by having his voice dubbed to million-dollar-epics, many of them classics. *Stagecoach* and *Red River* rank high in the list of great Westerns and *True Grit*, coming late in Wayne's career, revealed the grizzled veteran's mastery of his art. His portrayal of the profane, whiskey swigging, one-eyed marshal was characterized by some critics as a parody of Wayne's longtime screen character.

"Not so," said Wayne. "Rooster Cogburn's attitude toward life was maybe a little different, but he was basically the same character I've always played."

Although John Wayne enjoyed a career as a star without equal in movie history, there was never agreement about his talents as an actor. Wayne himself declared that he had never learned to act. "I don't act," he used to say. "I react. Regardless of character, I always play John Wayne."

Wayne was oversimplifying, as those who were in a position to judge were quick to point out. His colleagues had enormous respect for the range of his talents.

The effortlessness with which he dominated the screen was neither accidental nor the indifferent capacity of a tall guy dressed up in a cowboy suit. Wayne's size and athletic strength made him the ideal Western hero. More than that, he moved with a grace that ballet dancers could admire and he was able to speak the most banal dialogue with total conviction.

Audiences saw a lot of themselves in the image they knew so well on the screen. They'd watched him grow from a young, fair-skinned cowboy hero to a septugenerian whose craggy face mirrored their own. They knew an awful lot about Wayne's personal and professional life. With the same affection and admiration as his friends they called him "Duke."

They understood what Duke was talking about when he recalled the tough times of his early movie-making years during the Great Depression. And even in the best of times, when things ought to have looked their brightest, Duke often found himself knocked to the ground. These were the moments when his personal life had become a shambles or when his career prospects looked so bleak that he seriously considered switching his profession. But Duke, having been through it all before, simply picked himself up and started over again.

Wayne was neither a born loser nor a born winner. He was an ordinary human being who believed in fighting for what he wanted, whether it was the fulfill-

THE LEGACY OF A GIANT

By DAVID HANNA

ment of a professional ambition or simply a conviction. Americans have always admired men who stood on their own two feet. Duke embodied all the qualities of the American hero as well as the flaws of the guy next door. Because he was John Wayne his flaws stood out like huge warts on his craggy face. The very grandeur of his character defects—his arrogance, belligerence and stubbornness—endeared him to his fans.

John Wayne's legacy to future generations is a library of motion picture film without precedent in its commercial success or in its display of the artistry of one man. The possibility of so vast a collection of film ever being assembled by another motion picture actor is not within the realm of possibility. While Duke was battling the Big C a couple of pathetic old-timers stood tentatively in the wings ready to pick up whatever mythical title may exist for those who "made nearly as many movies as John Wayne."

Hopefully, they have packed up their shooting irons and returned to their TV commercials. Wayne did not become an American institution because of the numbers game. Yes, he made more movies than any major film actor in history, and he starred in vir-

tually all of them. His name stood above the title for nearly fifty years. When Wayne wasn't Number One in the roster of the ten top boxoffice stars he still held firm in the ranks of the first five. You can count on the fingers of your hands the Wayne movies which were duds.

"Americans love numbers, don't they?" an English newspaperman once remarked to me. "Why?"

I had no answer. Perhaps it had become a habit of American newspapering. Anyhow, I stopped collecting and attributing special importance to numbers. I began examining the events that created the numbers.

Wayne's durability was certainly extraordinary, but was it accidental? Hardly. Wayne was a brilliant motion picture actor who drew his artistry from a complex personality. He was far from the easygoing, genial, ever-lovin' personality that his publicity suggested. Moreover, Duke was the first to admit that he could be pretty mean and *ornery*. That he touched the emotions of his audiences as no other actor has ever managed was perhaps not as deliberate as his mastery of the screen.

Personally he was a lively extrovert with a great love of people. Inevitably he became excellent copy.

There was nothing mystical—or mythical—about Wayne. He was real. To avoid him you would have been obliged to move to another planet. Wayne stood tall in the saddle and out of it. Wherever he went he collected crowds. He loved them—and they loved him. Electricity sparked when Duke sat down with his fellow Americans. He was fully aware that many of them believed his face had already been carved on Mount Rushmore. What purpose would be served by disclaiming it? The illusion was part of his message—that they, like Duke and the presidents on Mount Rushmore, were privileged to live the American dream. Their minds could soar to the sky; their ambitions could be as wild and as outrageous as this limitless country of ours. Wayne knew because he lived to see his own dream come true.

Wayne was a big man. He stood tall. His arms were long. His stride was long. Like many big men he was graceful; like all strong men, he was gentle in physical contact. His handshake was firm, never bone-crunching. He was well-mannered. His voice lay in the middle register where it hung attractively in a lazy Midwestern drawl that came naturally to him.

Recently I read that in her memoirs one of Wayne's leading ladies will tell how she helped Duke with "the big words" in the dialogue of their picture. I can imagine it being believed. How easily we box people into stereotypes! The cowboys Duke played were more celebrated for their brawn than their brains. But be assured Duke never needed an adult reading course. He spoke cultivated English. Moreover, when Duke sounded off you could never accuse him of being dull.

Wayne was an articulate, thoughtful man who accepted the existence of enemies with the same grace that he welcomed the attention of his friends. Duke's controversial political beliefs were sincere, born of extensive reading and exposure to the thoughts and positions of men he admired. Duke put his money where his mouth was. He filmed two affirmations of his faith in America, *The Alamo* and *The Green Berets*, and spent years paying off the personal obligations he incurred in their financing. *The Alamo*, belatedly, has been "restudied" and has begun to edge into the realm of Wayne classics.

Even Hollywood's liberals had to admire Wayne's guts. On meeting him the new stars who knew Duke only from reading of the McCarthy era and the Hollywood Witch Hunt constantly expressed surprise at his charm and courtesy. He could make anyone feel comfortable and at home by the simple act of extending his hand and smiling with his bright blue eyes. Duke's code called for courtesy and professionalism even in dealing with political opponents.

Wayne was the consummate professional. Once he became a major Hollywood personality his roles, his life style and his image were molded to conform to Wayne's film character. He was the star who invented himself.

When you write about one "great" you begin to think of others. They used to say that Al Jolson didn't play to his audiences, that Jolie made love to them. Of Gary Cooper every director who worked with him claimed that Coop had an affinity for the camera unequalled by any other male star.

Wayne was neither a Jolson nor a Cooper. His talent had not come naturally. It developed slowly over the years. He was a late bloomer as a star—and it was even later before Hollywood gave him its long overdue respect.

With audiences it was different. Maybe Duke didn't make love to them. But he accomplished something just as important. He inspired their confidence and trust. They knew that as long as John Wayne was up there in charge everything was going to come out just fine.

I once asked Fannie Brice to describe her old friend Sophie Tucker. Fannie thought for a brief second. "She reminds me of a kid holding a balloon leading a parade on the Fourth of July."

That's how it was with John Wayne. He belonged to an era in America when kids *did* carry balloons and when they *did* march in Fourth of July parades, when patriotism was an emotion to be cherished—not lathered with cynicism.

Duke preferred the spirit of the America he had grown up in. And who knows but that Duke may have been right all along? Who knows but what a new century may diminish the *angst* afflicting our complicated world and we may discover that, as the Duke said, everything's going to be "real peachy after all"?

The Duke lived long enough to enjoy the honors that come wtih being an institution. An article, "the," went before his name—placing him in the same league with "the" President and "the" Pope. His political foes grew kinder. Duke had himself mellowed and supported the Panama Canal Treaty over the opposition of his old friend, Senator Barry Goldwater. Critics began to look at his old movies on television and abruptly discovered that Duke had improved a lot since the movies had first been released.

For his sake, I hope the movie buffs do not submit him to the wholesale dissection players like Bogart have endured. I doubt that anything more significant than the way the sun lay influenced Duke's kicking the grass with his left foot or right when there was that moment of silence as the hero sized up his adversary.

John Wayne belonged to that great era of Hollywood when movies were made to entertain and when star personalities were involved in nothing more complex than holding our attention while they searched for honesty, justice, love and happiness.

Sometimes Duke made out well. Sometimes he didn't.

That's how it went in his life—just as it did in ours.

That's why we care for him.

We are going to miss him. •

HIS OWN WORDS

Off screen or on, John Wayne had style. He was able to identify completely with the straight-talking characters he played. Wayne's real-life remarks, earned him as much attention as his performances. The following are typical of Duke's style:

"Fortunately, most of my crew has been with me for years and that makes things easier. They might be SOBs, but they're my SOBs."

"I figure legends are people who aren't around. Hell, I'm no legend. I'm here and planning to stay around a while longer."

"When I came into this business I had to learn how to say 'ain't.' Now it comes natural."

"Twilight years? If this is twilight, then hell, give me more."

"I'm 53 years old and 6'4". I've had three wives, five children and three grandchildren. I love good whiskey. I still don't understand women, and I don't think there is any man who does."

"I am proud of every day in my life I wake up in the United States of America."

"I always look for a story with basic emotions. A dog, a kid, a woman's love, a man's love. I've been in more bad pictures that just about anyone in the business."

"I know how to get my way. I don't argue. I become adamant."

"I licked the Big C. I caught it early. I don't care if I never sell another ticket at the boxoffice. I'd rather tell my story so some poor soul some place can get a check-up with his doctor and be as lucky as I was."

"There's a lot of yella bastards in the country who would like to call patriotism old-fashioned."

"I stopped getting the girl about ten years ago. It was just as well. By then I'd forgotten what I wanted to get the girl for." ■

Incredibly, John Wayne managed to drag himself from Newport to the 1979 Academy Awards ceremony where he made his last appearance, presenting the Best Picture Award to "The Deer Hunter."

WORLD MOURNS A PROUD AND COURAGEOUS AMERICAN

"We lost a big one, a jumbo in this business," said Bob Hope as news of the death of John Wayne spread throughout the world. "We knew he was in rough shape. But we kept our hopes up, because he had pulled through so many times before."

A hero on the screen, an extraordinary man in real life, a devoted father to his seven children, a deeply patriotic American, Wayne showed himself to be the stuff of which legends are made as, until the bitter end, he fought a sixteen-year long battle against the ravages of cancer. Wayne clung to life with the same rugged determination that he lived it.

Duke's seven children were at his bedside when the seventy-two-year-old star lapsed into a coma and died on June 11, 1979. "He had been in considerable pain," said Bernard Strohm, the administrator of the UCLA Medical Center in Los Angeles, "but he would not take much medication. He wanted to be awake when he died. He would tolerate the pain just to be near his family.

"Sometimes his vital signs would stabilize and he would look over and call, often in a loud voice for his children. When they would appear, he would lapse into a coma. It was the damndest thing. I have been

around teaching hospitals for twenty years and I've never seen anything like the love in that family."

John Wayne's first bout with cancer occurred in 1964 when he underwent surgery which removed one lung. Wayne, a heavy smoker, had been hospitalized under the usual security conditions which prevail when prominent personalities become seriously ill. But Wayne's prominence negated the best offers of his family and doctors to keep his condition secret. Having submitted to the consequences of his fame, Duke went public and, typically, he told the whole truth about his case. He volunteered for the public service announcements made by the National Cancer Society and for the next several years he utilized his fame to warn the public how to deal with the threat of the disease.

"It's hard to believe that John Wayne, the most durable of all films actors," said Charlton Heston, "is gone. But it's not surprising that to the end Duke gave an example of courage that made him more than an actor and a friend. He was—and is—an American institution."

When John Wayne entered the UCLA Medical Center on January tenth, he had already survived the removal of one lung and a heart bypass. His second bout with cancer began with what was first described as a routine gall bladder operation. Two days later his stomach was removed in an operation lasting nine and a half hours. A low-grade cancerous tumor was discovered.

Five days later, the hospital said that tissue tests revealed cancer in the gastric lymph nodes and a report noted that there was a "probability that the cancer would spread."

On learning the seriousness of his condition, city rooms around the world began what newspapers call "the death watch." Doctors confidently predicted that Duke would never leave the hospital alive. They pointed out that the operation was a drastic one. Everything surgically possible had been done for him. To apply chemotherapy at this point would amount to killing him. The general opinion was that the patient would be heavily sedated until his demise.

But Wayne fooled the experts. Amid reports that he was failing, Wayne's son, Patrick, said, "He's doing terrific" and a production associate, Tom Kane, said, "I saw him ... he's doing great. He's up and running around. His only problem is learning how to eat more slowly with his new stomach. He's learning to eat all over again. One of the reasons that they're holding him is that it takes a long time to learn the new process."

On February eleventh, a month after he'd entered UCLA Medical Center, the hospital announced that he'd slipped quietly out and had returned to his home at Newport Beach, thirty miles southeast of Los Angeles.

The Wayne compound at Newport where he could be close to his sons, daughters, their spouses and twenty-one grandchildren had become increasingly important to Duke in the last years of his life. There were ten rooms in the one-story ranch house which was situated on Newport Harbor and the Balboa peninsula. By Hollywood standards it was not especially luxurious, although it featured a pool, a library, a trophy room and a breathtaking view of the ocean. Its decor was the careful work of Pilar Palette, the Peruvian-born third wife of the star from whom he had never been divorced. His female companion at the time of his death was Pat Stacy, his secretary.

During his illnesses Pilar neither appeared at the hospital nor spoke with the press. She remained a model of discretion, just as she had been in the several years of their unexplained separation.

Regardless of the optimistic statements made by his sons who deplored pessimistic accounts of Duke's health, it was fairly obvious that Duke knew all along that he was dying. In dragging his cancer-ravaged body back to Newport, Duke was spending his last days exactly as he'd lived—to the hilt.

He was able to go sailing. He donned jogging togs, tied weights to his legs to support his frail body and tried running. His friends came to visit him and there was the family which remained within call day and night.

Duke wanted neither sympathy, tears, nor pity. It suited neither his image nor his own disposition to sit back and allow death to walk in through the window in the still of the night without putting up a fight. As it turned out, Duke waged one helluva fight—as tough as any he'd ever performed on the screen.

No one believed for an instant that John Wayne would appear at the Academy Awards to make a presentation—not even when the announcement was carried in the morning newspapers on the day of the ceremony in April.

But Duke was true to his promise. He drew an emotional standing ovation. Then he spoke. He said the ovation was "just about the only medicine a fellow'd ever really need. Believe me when I tell you that I'm still mighty pleased that I can amble down here tonight."

On April twenty-fifth Wayne was back in the hospital being treated for what was described as a slight bronchial condition. Ten days later it was announced that new cancer cells had been found in tissues removed from the actor's intestines.

Duke's last hospital stay enjoyed all the hoopla that marked his previous visits. Thousands of pieces of mail poured in from fans all over the world. There were telephone calls from famous people. Queen Elizabeth sent her greetings and President Carter paid the Duke a bedside visit. Following the fifteen-minute session, Carter said Wayne "was in good spirits ... made several jokes and thanked everybody for loving him so much."

A month before his death, Elizabeth Taylor and Maureen O'Hara appeared before a subcommittee of the House of Representatives urging Congress to approve a medal to be struck and presented to Wayne.

Miss O'Hara, who had costarred with Duke in several pictures, was tearful as she said, "I beg you to strike the medal, and it should just say one thing; 'John Wayne—American.' "

The idea of a medal for Wayne already enjoyed the support of President Carter who had written the committee that Wayne's "true grit helped win the Old West, World War II and thousands of our hearts." President Carter signed a bill on May 26, Wayne's birthday, authorizing the minting of a special medal.

Carter paid tribute to Wayne when, on learning of his death, he said, "In an age of few heroes, Duke was the genuine article."

Despite the fact that John Wayne grossed an estimated seven hundred million dollars over a fifty-year career and was one of the first stars to receive a percentage of a film's profits, the star's estate is not likely to cause either the Internal Revenue Service or California's tax collector to jump with joy. Wayne never amassed the millions that were collected by his contemporaries, Bob Hope, Bing Crosby and another cowboy star, Gene Autry.

However, he lived his last years in complete comfort. Holdings that have substantial value include

Wayne's cattle ranches in Arizona and his Newport Beach estate. There are also residuals in many of his pictures whose worth can not be estimated at this time.

The death of Elvis Presley was the previous high water-mark for press coverage of the passing of a theatrical celebrity until John Wayne. In the case of the older star the press was ready. Obituaries had been prepared months earlier and TV reporters cannily summoned Wayne's co-workers to the cameras to record their impressions while Duke was still alive.

Lauren Bacall, a political liberal, violently opposed to Duke and his colleagues in the Motion Picture Alliance for the Preservation of American Ideals, the group which spearheaded the Hollywood Witch Hunt, had been his costar in *The Shootist*.

She admitted fearing an encounter with Wayne. "I wondered if he would bring up the political past," she said on the MacNeil-Lehrer reports on the Public Broadcasting System. "Of course, he didn't," she went on. "Duke was the perfect gentleman. It would never occur to him to allow our political differences to affect the relationship necessary to successful movie-making."

Miss Bacall caught a side of Wayne seldom articulated by less perceptive friends of the star. Asked about his macho image, Bacall said in that authoritative voice of hers, "Frankly, I didn't see it. Far from being a macho, an aggressive male, I found him warm and very reserved. His good manners prevented him from being forward or, if you will, macho. Sometimes he would put his hand on mine. He did it quietly. He was very gentle."

Duke was not fond of funerals. He'd attended too many of his old friends' last rites to inflict the burden of a ceremony on his survivors. He often said, "When I go, shove me in an oven somewhere, burn me and toss the ashes wherever it's convenient. When it's over I'd like my friends to get together, sit down and hoist a few for me. That would do it—just fine."

And how would Duke like to be remembered? He liked that question.

"Affectionately," he said, "by my friends. As for anyone else they're welcome to think anything they like. It certainly won't matter to me then."

On the eve of his father's private funeral, Michael Wayne said, "Dad lived with simple dignity and wanted his funeral services conducted the same way."

Those who wanted to honor the actor were urged to make contributions to the newly created John Wayne Memorial Cancer Fund—a project which was discussed during the last two weeks of Duke's life. A hospital spokesman said, "Mr. Wayne was enthusiastic about it, and he talked about it with the hospital and with his children."

The press of the world joined America in paying tribute to John Wayne and one Japanese newspaper ran as its banner, *Mr. America Is Dead*. It was taken for granted that readers would identify their friend and old favorite John Wayne through his nickname.●

Pat Stacy, identified by Pilar Palette as her husband's "secretary," became the star's steady date during the last years of his life.

Maureen O'Hara, Duke's frequent costar, sheds tears as she asks a House subcommittee to authorize a special gold medal for John Wayne. The medal, as she suggested, has been struck with the words, "John Wayne—American."

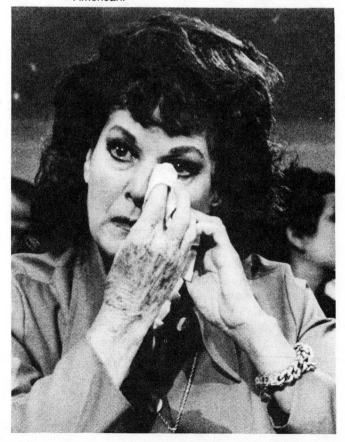

A Kid Named "Duke"

HIS WAS A LONELY CHILDHOOD—AND HIS
HABIT OF RUNNING AWAY FROM HOME WAS A
SOURCE OF CONSTANT DISMAY TO HIS PARENTS.

As far as John Wayne was concerned his life began in 1927 when, still a student at the University of Southern California on a football scholarship, he landed a summer job at the old Fox Studios as a grip. The job had been "laid on" for him by the university's football coach, Dean Jones, whose relationship with the Hollywood great started at the top. Besides being a popular coach, a man-about-town, Jones' inside pocket usually carried a supply of choice tickets to the games. Since box seats on the fifty-yard line were as desirable then as they are now, Jones was someone to be cultivated. In those nonunion days of movie making it was fairly simple to do him a favor—like putting his players to work to supplement their scholarships.

Tom Mix, the fabled cowboy star who earned and spent seventeen thousand dollars a week, and George Marshall, a director, provided Duke with his first studio pass. Wayne's salary was thirty-five dollars a week, big pay at the time, more than young lawyers were making and not much less than the salaries paid assistant bank managers.

Even if years later Wayne could recall every detail of that first meeting with Tom Mix in the star's dressing room, the numerous photos of Mix on the walls, the star's decision that Wayne and another USC footballer would help him keep in shape by running two or three miles a day, the fact remains that there was once a kid named "Duke." John Wayne wasn't always a *Living Legend*. He was born, an ordinary red-faced baby, twenty years before that summer's day when Mix shooed him off to George Marshall's office with the promise that "he'll keep you busy until I'm ready."

You couldn't say that Wayne ignored his youth. He simply "wrote around" it. Wayne chose to embroider the happy days, ignored his youthful loneliness, his childish jealousy of a younger brother, the fact that making friends was difficult for him and that his habit of running away from home was a source of constant dismay to his parents. Years later his mother, Mary Brown Morrison, would smile and say, "I always did the right thing. There was nothing else a decent person could do."

To those who understood, Mary was referring to the strained relationship that haunted her marriage to Wayne's father, Clyde L. Morrison, a pharmacist who bore the inevitable nickname,

"Doc." Mary Morrison had waited until Duke reached maturity and had begun making his own way in the world before seeking a long overdue divorce from Doc.

From all accounts, Clyde Morrison was fairly typical of Midwestern men of his time, above average actually, since he had mastered a profession. Clyde knew farming, was a fair enough handyman but most important, he understood the "give and take" of life. He lived through good times and bad with equal aplomb and, as Americans always have, he dreamed of a better tomorrow.

His easy acceptance of fate conflicted with Mary's ambitions for her family and arguments between his parents became so much a part of life that their son's only release lay in running away, spending nights in freight trains near their home or, when he grew older, in reading his way through the shelves of libraries, losing himself in the works of Richard Harding Davis, Kipling, James Fenimore Cooper, everything dealing with American history and the opening up of the West.

Then, when he was able to earn spending money, he discovered the movies. Besides Tom Mix, there were other idols whose heroics on the screen seized his imagination—George O'Brien (who later became his friend), Harry Carey (whom Wayne dramatically befriended after he'd become a star), Buck Jones, Ken Maynard, Hoot Gibson, Fred Thompson. They were the great cowboy stars—today mere footnotes in the glamorous history of Hollywood. But six decades ago, they were the heroes kids worshipped. They taught them that there were good guys and bad guys—and the good guys always won. Evil was punished with a fusillade of bullets, by hanging, by battling to the death at the edge of a cliff—occasionally, by a jury.

For years the Western was the staple of the American movie—for good reason. The opening of the West was the story of individual heroics, pioneers fighting for their existence, the Indian scout braving hostile territory, the marshal who brought law to the land, and heroes who rescued maidens in distress.

It dramatized a world and ideals to which a young, impressionable kid could easily relate. Especially one who was already in love with the outdoors, a boy to whom riding was as natural as walking, a romantic who needed to be lifted out of the depressing atmosphere that suffocated him at home—the eternal bickering of his father and mother, their despairing quest for the pot of gold at the end of the rainbow and the tragedy of watching their love slowly tarnish until it turned to bitter hatred.

Throughout his starring years—and even earlier—Wayne remained selective about the details of his youth, obviously feeling that the picture of a troubled boy, awkward physically, insecure emotionally, was ill-suited to the carefully cultivated Wayne image, the all-American super-hero with a will of iron and nerves of steel.

In recalling his parents, Wayne, understandably, glossed over their imperfections to describe them as hard-working, honest, God-fearing folks, which undoubtedly they were. Mary had been born in County Cork, Ireland; Clyde was a native of Iowa. She was a telephone operator when they met in Des Moines and Clyde was a druggist.

Mary Brown is believed to have been the aggressor in the courtship. They were married in Knoxville, Iowa, on September 29, 1905. Their first son, whom they named Marion, was born on May 26, 1907 in Winterset, Iowa, where Clyde was working in the local drug store. Another son, Robert, was born a year later.

Mary Brown and Clyde Morrison were such opposites that, according to the rule, their attraction should have been exciting and fulfilling. It wasn't.

Mary's frugality, her aggressiveness and skill at pushing her easy-going husband along professionally served both of them well at first. They managed to save enough money for Doc Morrison to buy his own drug store. It flourished because people were attracted to Doc. He was tall and handsome, an athlete who'd played football at college. He possessed a fine baritone voice which, in spite of his shyness, Doc let go at various town functions. The Morrisons built a splendid house and might have become a solid family unit had their ambitions been more alike.

Clyde wanted to enjoy life. He liked attending football games, coaching the kids and being part of the community. His customers were his friends. Many, knowing Doc was a soft touch, overextended their credit. He was taken advantage of in other ways, and Mary's sharp Irish temper flared. Their arguments were loud and constant, accounting for Marion's insecurity. He was afraid to sleep in the dark and there were periods in his young life when he couldn't sleep at all.

When Doc discovered that he had tuberculosis he followed his doctor's advice to leave Iowa and move to a more suitable climate. Doc decided on Southern California. The Morrisons sold their home and store in Winterset. Mary and the children moved in with her family in Des Moines while Doc traveled to California to homestead in

Duke was believed to have been four or five years old when this picture was taken. The other lad is not identified.

Palmdale, California.

Doc acquired ninety acres, put up a small house, little more than a cabin, and began to farm the land. Mary, Marion and Robert joined him in 1914.

For Mary, the harsh desert life was an impossibility and an imposition on her background, her role as wife and mother and a threat to her ambitions. She sensed disaster at the outset, which contributed little to the harmony and support that a man needed in order to pioneer. Clyde's health had improved considerably, but the desert affected Mary. She fought a losing battle against its perils—insects, rattlers, dust storms, all the other inconveniences. There was no running water and after living in a handsome gabled home, the idea of an outdoor privy offended Mary.

Young Marion began to come out of his shell. To attend school at Palmdale Marion had to walk four miles each way. Sometimes he rode one of the two horses Doc was able to acquire. Wayne liked to remember riding to school and how his imagination would soar as he identified with pioneers of the Old West who may have taken this same road a generation or two earlier.

Young Marion enjoyed working side by side with his father and he could spin hair-raising tales of how close they came to meeting their doom when they stumbled upon an angry rattler and how they battled the jackrabbits that afflicted their crops. He loved to quote his father's advice: "Always keep your word. A gentleman never insults anyone intentionally. Don't look for trouble, but if you get into a fight, make sure you win it." Wayne then explained how he'd improved on his father's philosophy, "A gentleman never insults anyone *unintentionally.*"

As Wayne pieced it together, life on the desert was the sort of battle against the elements that tested a youth's strength and molded his character. In this sense it was. Still, Marion had his problems at home—and away from home. He was "different" to the other kids—"different" in the usual sense. He spoke a strange language, his manners were different, refined by the small town life he knew and those of his parents. He was skinny, gangling and awkward. He often walked a mile or so out of his way to the Palmdale school to avoid the taunting of the other pupils. Young Marion Morrison was no hero then; he artfully practiced his father's advice of avoiding trouble.

Marion was nine years old when the Morrisons called it quits and moved to Glendale where Doc was able to find a low paying job in a drug store. Twice in his short span of life, Marion had been uprooted and it was difficult for him to understand the reasons why. Not that there was much time to. The family needed money and Marion got a newspaper route so his pennies could go into the family pot. He was old enough to realize that his family's situation had worsened.

For Marion the desert had worked its magic. The battle against nature, the very real danger of rattlers, the threat of storms, the constant disasters he watched his father meet with complete calm had molded a self-reliant youngster who began to lose his fears and subconsciously realized that in his own pursuits he might find escape from the worsening situation at home. At one point Mary had packed up and returned to Des Moines. But she could not bear the separation from her children and returned. As she said, "I did the right thing."

Glendale was far from the thriving city it is today. Rather, in the period the Morrisons lived there it was virtually a prairie. There were wide open spaces between clumps of houses and small businesses—open land that offered excellent facilities to the movie companies. A couple of them had their offices in Glendale.

Offices? One could hardly call them that. What did a movie company need? Nothing more than a couple of shacks and a telephone line. Here the producer could huddle with his director and work out the day's schedule while the paymaster sat behind a walled-off section with a safe beside him and a list of people to be paid at the end of the day. The movie business was a fly-by-night affair requiring cash on the barrelhead to survive. Crews, supporting actors, extras and even the handful of stars that existed at the time were paid by the day.

So Marion's horizons broadened. Besides the paper route, his school work, the library, the movies, there was actual movie-making to be watched. He recalled having particular admiration for Helen Holmes, the serial star, who was her own stunt woman. Her home was a mile or so away from the Morrisons' and Marion often got to see her close up as she galloped around Glendale on her Palomino. She was a superb horsewoman.

In growing into adolescence, Marion changed from an awkward, small town kid into a handsome, attractive youth. From a shy, nervous boy he was transformed into a tall, husky youth who became the idol of Glendale High School,

president of his class, a star football player, an all-around popular student.

Marion's first ambition was to match his father's hope for him to become a United States Naval Officer. He got as far as an alternative appointment to Annapolis. It didn't work out. So Marion went the next best route—looking for an athletic scholarship at college. He was a good football player. Young Marion enjoyed the sport. It was rugged and tough, a contact sport, a man-to-man encounter that fitted his ideal of physical courage.

The University of Southern California accepted him and the only speculation possible at this point is what might have become of Marion Morrison if the family hadn't moved to Glendale. Everything that happened to the college footballer in those two years at USC was accidental.

Tom Mix was someone to know. He was a friendly man—even if he never stepped out of character. His tailor-made Western outfits were one color only—white. He wore them everywhere to social functions, premieres, on his numerous world tours, to the White House. He drove long, custom-made white cars, convertibles, so his tanned smiling face was always visible. Mix embodied all the outward appearances that success in Hollywood suggested. He was rich, famous and loved. Everyone catered to him and, in the grand manner of a star who knew success could be capricious and depended on his·public, Mix was gentle, gracious and charming. Morrison may not have dreamed that one day his own career would prove more dazzling and long-lived than Mix's, but a lot of the Wayne image was born either subconsciously or deliberately from his association with Tom Mix.

Not that they got around to "running three miles a day" to keep Mix in shape. Morrison couldn't. He was too busy. George Marshall, an up and coming director, found plenty for him to do. Wayne remembered it all well. "In those days you could operate in every department of pictures. You didn't need a union card. I was a carpenter. I was a juicer. I rigged lights. Carried props. Hauled furniture. I got to know the nuts and bolts of picture making. That is why I know what a scene is going to look like on the film. I don't have to look at the daily rushes. I never do. At that time all I wanted to be was the best property man in the business. A chief property man could get a hundred and fifty a week—a lot of money."

With Marion firmly ensconced at Fox in what looked like a steady job, Mary and Doc Morrison finally divorced. Each married again, evidently to mates more compatible to their attitudes. His mother lived a long life but the father he idolized died in 1938 of a heart attack, just a year before *Stagecoach,* the film that put Wayne on the road to international stardom. There was, however, the satisfaction of seeing his son launched on a totally unexpected career.

Wayne was photogenic but he wasn't aware of it. It's a quality that can't be acquired. An actor is either born with an affinity for the camera or not. Being photogenic is an intangible and often has nothing to do with looks. There have been the Garbos and Merle Oberons, Ava Gardners and Elizabeth Taylors who could never be photographed badly. Among males there were Rudolph Valentino, Robert Taylor, Tyrone Power, Gary Cooper and today's Robert Redford. But there have been flawed stars as well, artists who could look breathtakingly beautiful on the screen and quite ordinary away from the camera. They also possessed the intangible called "photogenic."

Young Morrison got his first chance in front of the cameras because Fox had more football players on its payroll than a studio that needed them for a movie. Warners was filming a Richard Barthelmess picture *The Drop Kick* and Morrison was shipped across town to play a member of the team. He wasn't particularly pleased by the loan-out. However, he took a brighter view of the acting profession when he caught sight of his paycheck. In a couple of days he'd earned more than twice as much as he did working as a prop man.

But Morrison knew the hazards of the acting profession better than most. The precariousness of the profession bothered him. He preferred steady work. He'd become friends with George O'Brien, who encouraged him to keep his hand in acting. "You've always got prop work or carpentry to fall back on. You're the sort of kid that can make out whatever the situation."

Morrison heeded the star's advice, depending on chance for his next crack at an actor's check. It came when he was assigned to a John Ford movie called *Mother Machree.*

At the time Ford was a young director, not yet in George Marshall's league. But he'd been around the business long enough to have earned the reputation as a "no nonsense" film man who knew his stuff and could get it on film fast, efficiently, with quite a bit of imagination and a minimum of editing. Ford cut his film in his head as he went along.

For *Mother Machree* Ford had built a huge outdoors set, an Irish rural scene. To give it an authentic touch he brought in a large flock of geese. It was a good idea except that when they weren't needed, the geese waddled freely around the set getting in everybody's way. Looking around him, Ford saw Morrison's Irish face and pulled him off his prop job and sent him to wardrobe for a costume as goose herder.

Ford, who had played football himself, got to talking to Morrison, calling him "goose herder" for want of knowing his name. By the end of the picture the two men were friends. Over the years they were to merge their talents in filming some of their most memorable films. Another player in *Mother Machree* as Victor McLaglen who also became close to Morrison and the director.

Ford may not have known then what he was doing at the time but eventually it became clear that from this coterie of friendships developed early in his career, John Ford was developing the group of actors who performed in his pictures year after year—the John Ford stock company. Their talents, then minimal, expanded as Ford's vision of movie making grew and with it his stature and individuality as a director.

With the breakup in his family a reality, young Morrison was on his own—a new adventure that he really didn't relish. In spite of their faults the Morrisons had sustained a home for their children, kept them clothed, saw to it that they received good educations and genuinely loved them. Being alone brought a sense of uneasiness that he'd not known before.

In John Ford, Morrison found a surrogate father. Theirs was a relationship that continued until Ford died. Ford's strength and self-confidence rubbed off on Ford's friends, Morrison particularly.

Marion Morrison had taken his nickname "Duke" to college and to Fox. It came from a dog he owned when he was delivering newspapers and as far as he was concerned, being Duke Morrison suited him fine. Since he received no billing in the first pictures it really didn't matter. He was usually part of the crowd, a football player, a chauffeur, a goose herder. He'd worked as a bit player in about eight pictures, three with John Ford, who admired the inexperienced youth but had never given second thoughts to working him into larger parts.

Duke was just part of the gang—men like Ward Bond, Victor McLaglen, Bruce Cabot and George O'Brien, who fashioned themselves into an informal club of boozing, brawling toilers in the movie industry. Rank didn't bother Ford—nor did it appear to affect O'Brien's friendship with the young football player.

However, Duke Morrison hadn't gone unnoticed as he wandered around Fox, doing his bit parts or working as a prop man. Raoul Walsh, another director, wondered about the young man's potential as an actor. Hollywood was constantly on the alert for new faces in this era of its history and Walsh was preparing a biggie that he foresaw could have a great many problems. They began at the top—in the casting of the leading man.

Walsh was an old-timer in the business, having started his career as an actor in 1910 when he performed in D.W. Griffith two-reelers. He had played John Wilkes Booth in *The Birth Of A Nation.* He had turned to directing in 1918 and continued as one of Hollywood's major creative men until 1964, when he retired.

Walsh had made the switch from silents to talkies with comparative ease. In the transition to movies that talked, the Western had temporarily gone into limbo because the sound equipment was incapable of working under outdoor conditions. Microphones were concealed on the sets of the early talkies, concealed in various positions, behind chairs, in vases, behind mirrors, etc. Cameras had to be placed in soundproofed booths because their whirring noise could be picked up.

However, sound had progressed sufficiently by 1930 that Winfield Sheehan, the production head for William Fox, decided it was time to attempt a big-scale outdoor drama with sound. It may have been the right time from a technical viewpoint, but it turned out to be bad judgment otherwise—notwithstanding the fact that Walsh had already proved the point with *In Old Arizona*, starring Warner Baxter as the *Cisco Kid*. It was a comparatively static picture, heavy on dialogue for a Western, but Walsh had managed some excellent action scenes and authentic, if uneven, sound effects by using portable equipment similar to that employed by the newsreel companies.

The Big Trail was to have none of the flaws found in *Arizona*. There would be no hoofbeats fading in and out—but a steady clippety-clop. Bullets would wizz through the air and sound like bullets. Morever, the actors' diction would be clear. This was promised by the cast supporting Gary Cooper, originally intended for the lead, consisting of Broadway actors, each a master in crisp diction: Ian Keith, Tully Marshall and Tyrone Power, Sr. The leading lady, who knew how to talk, was Marguerite Churchill. To further insure that the actors would properly sound their consonents and open their vowels, Sheehan hired an English character actor, Lumsden Hare, as dialogue director.

For icing on the cake Sheehan and William Fox had been sold on a large-screen 70mm process called Grandeur. The studio owner put his own name in front of it and it became known as Fox Grandeur. To the few who saw it, *The Big Trail,* in wide screen and color, foreshadowed the technical heights the screen would achieve two decades later with the perfection of Cinemascope, Panavision, Todd A-O and all the other wide-screen techniques.

The lead, a frontier scout, was a natural for Cooper whose loan-out had already been arranged. But canny Samuel Goldwyn, aware that William Fox was in serious financial trouble and betting on *The Big Trail* to bail him out, took a second look at the situation. It didn't please him. He pulled Cooper out of the deal and started his own production of *The Winning of Barbara Worth,* the film which accomplished for "Coop" what *Stagecoach* would do nine years later for John Wayne.

Hundreds of thousands of dollars were tied up in the production when Samuel Goldwyn landed his haymaker. Walsh tested literally every Western star in the business, knowing eventually he would have to compromise for one of them. Then it happened. Duke Morrison was going about his job, stripped to the waist. Walsh asked Ford about Morrison. He thought a second and answered, "Why not test him?"

Walsh called Wayne into his office, told him to let his hair grow because he was being considered for the lead in *The Big Trail*. Duke was only midly impressed, and even less so after enduring the rigors that were to prepare him for the test—learning to throw tomahawks and knives and taking diction lessons.

Wayne described it this way to English film writer Mike Tomkies:

"So I learned to throw the knives and tomahawks. Then I went to this wonder coach from New York who was going to teach everyone how to act. Now I'd already seen this guy ruin a picture with Vic McLaglen and Myrna Loy. He made a 150-foot scene, all just talk, talk, talk, with all these beautiful words. This great director had been helping Ford out when he couldn't be there and I'd seen just what he'd done. I didn't even want to go and prop for the director if he could do that to Ford, so I had a dim view of him before I went to any of his private lessons. He was all very dramatic in his talk, all psuedo-Shakespearean, and his idea of western dialogue was 'Greetings. Great Bear, tell the Great White Mountain hello for me,' all in great round vowels. He made me make sweeping gestures with my arms and mince up and down theatrically. I took about two weeks of that; then I just quit going to him."

Wayne's film test was almost catastrophic. He made it with Tyrone Power, Sr., who was one of the great Shakespearean actors of the day. Marguerite Churchill and Ian Keith were theatre names. They were positioned on the set near a covered wagon.

Walsh told Duke, "You're playing the leading scout of a wagon train heading West. There are no lines for you to learn. They'll just throw questions at you about the trip. Don't try to act. Just react naturally, as if it were happening in real life."

But the actors *had* read the script. And they started hurling questions at Wayne. How long is the trip? Where will we eat? Will we see any buffaloes? Will we be attacked by Indians? Wayne started tripping over his own tongue and felt like a clumsy oaf.

He took the questioning from the girl and from Tyrone Power, but when Keith started in on him, Wayne got mad—something he hadn't planned to do at all. He lost his temper and began hurling

In his teens John Wayne, who was still
Marion Morrison, began to change from an
awkward, gangling kid, to a tall, handsome
young fella with an infectious grin, clear
blue eyes and a mop of unruly black hair.

questions back at Keith.

"Don't say any more! Where you from, mister? Why are you goin' West? Can you handle a rifle? You got pale hands, you sure as hell don't look the pioneering sort to me."

Then Keith got confused and started to stammer, and Wayne thought this time he'd *really* blown it. He'd fixed Keith, but he'd ruined himself, too. Then suddenly Walsh shouted out in delight.

"Cut! He'll do!" Wayne had the role. Suddenly he was the star of a two-million-dollar spectacular. Star? His salary was seventy-five dollars a week—and *The Big Trail* didn't exactly blaze any trails for Wayne.

To show the film, theatres had to buy bigger screens and "squeeze" lenses to fit onto their normal projectors. The lenses would throw out bigger images. It was a practical idea, certainly, but during the depression most theatres couldn't afford the extra expense.

Depression admission prices were low. At first run theatres in New York audiences could see the latest feature films, a stage show, hear huge orchestras like Paul Whiteman's, watch a newsreel and a short subject for thirty-five cents before noon. The price scale rose to just under a dollar at night.

When movies reached the neighborhood houses, only posh theatres dared charge as much as fifty cents. The average night time admission ranged between twenty-five and forty cents. Then there were the bread-and-butter houses where kids caught the Saturday matinee for a dime—two features, a serial, an Our Gang comedy, sometimes two short comedies.

The Big Trail, which insiders at Fox called *The Big Drunk* because of its cast of heavy drinkers, ended up a big flop. It led to the bankruptcy of William Fox and to charges of fraud which sent him to jail. Eventually the assets of Fox were assembled by Darryl Zanuck and Joseph Schenk, who formed 20th Century-Fox.

One positive result of *The Big Trail* was the creation of Duke's name. At first the Duke objected to changing it at all. He liked his name. Morrison had a lot of history behind it. Two uncles had fought on the Union side in the Civil War and there were ancestors who could be traced back—with various degrees of distinction—to 1800.

He was utterly unself-conscious about Marion being a female as well as a male name. Marion was used by far more men at the time; it was fairly common in his part of the world. Once he conceded to Wayne, there came the problem of choosing his first name. Anthony was rejected by Sheehan because "it was too Italian." Finally they settled on John.

But after *The Big Trail* had flopped, down the drain went all the hoopla about the hot new discovery. Wayne went to New York for personal appearances and tried to live up to the biography publicists at Fox had manufactured for him. They created the image of a star football player, an all-American, the dashing romantic who'd dated every girl in Hollywood. They really poured it on.

Wayne made two more pictures under the Fox contract to which Walsh had signed him, *Girls Demand Excitement* and *Three Girls Lost.* They weren't the worst movies ever made and in the long run they probably helped him. His name had stayed alive and Wayne was signed to a contract within a week of being dropped by Fox. He was on salary at Columbia.

He made one film, *Arizona.*

Over the years there have been many tall stories about the problems Wayne encountered at Columbia. They centered around Harry Cohn, the despotic studio head who ran the plant as his own private empire, brooking no interference. To make sure his serfs were totally in his control, Cohn established an elaborate network of spies—and wasn't beyond spying himself. So the Wayne-Cohn myths have grown and they can be taken for what they're worth.

One story had it that they found Duke drunk and sleeping it off one morning on the back lot. Another said that he'd been fooling around with Harry Cohn's private playmate of the moment. Either could be true. It might also have been that maybe, one day, the Duke just didn't show enough deference when he said, "Good morning." Cohn was the kind of executive who would fire a man because he didn't like the color of his necktie.

Cohn's dislike for Wayne enlarged to a positive hatred. When option time came, he met the contract clause that raised Duke's salary to three hundred and fifty dollars a week but he spotted him in supporting roles in the two series Columbia was making at the time—westerns starring Buck Jones and Tim McCoy. He also cast him as a crooked football player and loaned him out to Universal for minor parts. This was Cohn's technique of punishment.

But it wasn't all waste. Everywhere John Wayne went he learned something new. In *The Big Trail* he'd done his own stunts—and Walsh encouraged him. Said Walsh some years later, "He was never the brainiest guy in the business, but he was a kid who kept his word, pretty unusual for an actor. He was always on time, knew what was expected of him and if he didn't know how to do something, he'd ask. That was also pretty unusual."

Working with old pros like Buck Jones and Tim McCoy was in itself an education. Wayne started taking acting seriously. He'd always ridden, but now he learned horsemanship as a skill.

In retrospect the tough time Harry Cohn had given him may have been the break of his life—even if it landed him on Poverty Row.

Saddlin' Up on Poverty Row

POVERTY ROW WAS WHERE THEY GROUND OUT THE B-PICTURES—
THE QUICKIES, THE CHEAPIES AND THE WESTERNS!

Marguerite Churchill was Wayne's leading lady in "The Big Trail," which should have made him a star. Instead, Duke headed for Poverty Row.

Although many stars, including two of the greatest of silent films, William Farnum and Henry B. Walthall, ended up on Poverty Row, as did Kay Francis, the first female star of the talkies to be paid ten thousand dollars a week, the reverse has happened only once.

The single super-star to come out of Poverty Row was John Wayne. And to compound the irony, there is the fact that Wayne became the superstar of all time, the biggest single moneymaker in the history of the motion picture business. His pictures are believed to have earned more than five hundred million dollars. No male star ever came close to equaling his record for longevity or continual appeal. Some of Duke's pictures have earned less money than others, but not since *The Big Trail* did he ever bear the ignominy of a flop.

It is as useless to ponder the hypothetical question of whether there would have been a John Wayne without Povery Row as it is to consider what Marion Morrison might have become had his family never moved to Glendale.

Of one thing we can be sure. Poverty Row afforded Wayne an opportunity to hone his craft, to master the acting trade and to develop the Wayne characterization to a degree that might never have been possible in the major studios. The very nature of the pictures that came out of Poverty Row—their cheapness and need for resourceful stars like Wayne—provided him with an extraordinary opportunity to be his own man.

Poverty Row allowed—even encouraged—John Wayne to create John Wayne. He began to polish and perfect the actor's tricks so strongly associated with him: the stylized walk as he entered into one showdown after the other; clenching his teeth when angered; tucking his chin into his neck and sporting his sheepish cow-eyed look when being admonished by someone; and the wide-eyed, almost mugging

look of surprise when an unexpected punch landed from an antagonist. These were the mannerisms that formed a Wayne characterization.

None of it came easily. Wayne practiced for hours in front of a mirror affecting the walk, the squint, the swing of the arms and other body movements that identified him as the virile "good guy."

Wayne's image was spun from both personal and artificial ingredients. His big advantage lay in the fact that he looked the part. Wayne was tall (6'4") and lean. He rode well. He looked fast with a gun. Off screen he admitted he couldn't hit a barn door at close range. He paid attention to his costume, always wearing tailored trousers and beautifully styled shirts. When everything was put together—the gait, the eyes, the lean, rugged body, the clothes—we recognized our ideal hero. Wayne personified honesty, sincerity, loyalty, rugged determination and courage, all touched with compassion.

On Poverty Row he was allowed to tinker with the Western stereotype. He avoided wearing the customary white garb of the hero. He wasn't above taking a careful drink now and then. He sometimes gave the leading ladies what they were asking for—a kiss. His juvenile fans didn't seem to mind.

Newspapermen over the years carefully examined John Wayne and heard him tell, both with affection and horror, of his days on Poverty Row. But for all his capacities as a story teller, even Wayne would have admitted that explaining Poverty Row to someone who'd never been there represented quite a challenge.

The Row was a fascinating product of its times, the Depression. It existed to fill a need that the major studios overlooked in their zeal to capitalize on sound. They neglected the Western as they turned their studios over to the singing

*This is a
rare publicity
shot of young
John Wayne
in which
he's demonstrating
the proper
way of throwing
a knife—a
skill Duke had
to master for
"The Big Trail"*

and dancing stars like Dick Powell, Ruby Keeler, Jeanette MacDonald, Nelson Eddy, Grace Moore and a host of others who came to conquer the medium of sound.

The giants of the sagebrush, Tom Mix and Buck Jones, were turned out to pasture. They went on the road, appearing in circuses. So did Colonel Tim McCoy. Fred Thompson died at the peak of his career. Bob Steele drifted into character roles, as did Jack Holt. Dustin Farnum died and William Farnum, once listed on studio payrolls at ten thousand dollars a week, was picking up peanuts wherever he could find them. Rin-Tin-Tin failed to survive the talkie era.

But the Western turned out to be more durable than the major studios realized. It had been taken over by independent producers who lured Buck Jones, Ken Maynard and George O'Brien back to the old corral. They might also have revived the career of Tom Mix had he not met an untimely death in 1937 in an automobile accident.

By the time I arrived in Hollywood as a young newspaperman in the mid-thirties, Westerns again were plentiful. The popularity of the double bill required Hollywood to produce an enormous number of movies annually, thus creating the low budget B picture and the quickie Western. Only three studios carried "oateater" inventory: Columbia, Universal and Paramount. The last did not produce but released the *Hopalong Cassidys* of producer Harry Sherman.

Virtually all the bread-and-butter Westerns were independently produced out of an area surrounding Gower Street and Sunset Boulevard known as Poverty Road. The intersection, called Gower Gulch, centered around the Columbia drug store, a nearby liquor store, a Western-style bar with whiskey at two-bits a shot, and several shops selling Western outfits, holsters, boots, large leather belts and other paraphernalia—all manufactured in New York City and New Jersey.

Small offices, seldom larger than two rooms, store fronts actually, identified the various companies operating along Poverty Row—Chesterfield Pictures, Ambassador Pictures, Monogram, Tiffany, Resolute, Beacon, Majestic and Mascot Films. Unlike older companies tied to familiar trademarks, bright Art Deco signatures with intricate designs and lots of chrome shooting stars and rockets identified the various inhabitants of Poverty Row.

The area's nickname told it all. When Tom Mix died, the era of the millionaire-cowboy star ended. Buck Jones had saved his loot but when he worked afterward it was at a fraction of his old salary. New names were coming up in the Western field and Poverty Row producers were a hard lot to bargain with.

Poverty Row fascinated me and since my first job involved representing a movie trade paper catering to small town and neighborhood exhibitors, I covered it extensively, even developing an affection for it. I had the field to myself. I knew all the producers and picked up extra money by writing their press books. The first story I wrote for the New York *Times* dealt with the wonders of Poverty Row—the double dealing, production short-cuts, and all the tricks that were part of making acceptable movies in six days at budgets seldom exceeding five thousand dollars. Many veterans of old Hollywood, including Carl Laemmle, are credited with the phrase, but it was Mr. Stern, father of the Stern Brothers, among the better quickie producers, who said, "A tree is a tree, a rock is a rock, shoot it in Griffith Park."

None of the producers owned anything. To make their films they rented, borrowed or stole—everything from sound stages to livestock, location areas, and costumes for the women. The Gulch cowboys brought their own. Western Electric, owning all the patents on sound equipment, permitted an independent sound company to operate freely in the Gulch, thus avoiding monopoly charges. There were no guilds; writers took what they were offered for a script and at the larger indies, writers' pay never exceeded two hundred dollars a week. Directors' salaries ranged between $500 and $750 a week and star salaries seldom went above one thousand—which meant a thousand a picture.

Financing was precarious and depended largely on the good will of distributors, known as States Rights distributors, who handled most of the independents. Since rentals for quickie product ranged between five and ten dollars a day, the producer's share of the dollar never produced the cash flow he needed. He remained in a constant state of debt to the States Rights franchise holders for advances. Sometimes an angel would come along or a couple of bold young men, dreaming of becoming, like Columbia, an "independent major," would try to float stock. In the thirties, investors had had it with issues marked "highly speculative." They refused to nibble. City Marshalls marched in and out of Poverty Row constantly, sealing off "attached property," consisting of vintage typewriters and battered desks barely worth a junkman's visit.

Men brash enough to take on monopolies had no trouble slapping people around; not with a depression on.

But the Guilds were standing in the wings, and by 1938 the halycon days of five dollar extras or family and friends playing extras for "fun" were over. The Screen Actors Guild won its first contract.

Nevertheless Gulch cowboys still were grateful to pick up $25 a day for bit parts and villains could be bought for $200. You never worried about the girl, usually a newcomer, whose salary was a standard two hundred.

Noah Beery, brother of Wallace and a fine actor in his own right, star of *Chu Chin Chow,* a long-run musical in New York and London, once accepted a thousand dollars for a single day's work. It lasted about eighteen hours, but Beery didn't complain until he saw the picture. The director had shot Beery in key scenes showing him as the mastermind of a band of outlaws. A hooded double played the rest of the Beery part, reading lines that Beery had made on "wild track."

Quickie producers were vastly more resourceful than the majors. Paramount, for example, sent beautiful Isa Miranda packing and back to Italy because of her accent. No one thought to dub the excellent actress until her English improved. The studio threw a valuable property and a million dollars down the drain. That could never have happened on Poverty Row.

I remember being at the Alexander Brothers' office when a call came late in the afternoon that the generator on location had failed. With the brothers I raced out to the Valley to find the director serenely winding up the day's work with light to spare. He'd lined up all the trucks and cars belonging to the company, placed them in a key position, turned on their headlights and told the cameraman, "Roll 'em."

Indoor fight scenes were saved for Saturday night, the last day of shooting, when, instead of a dollar for eating money, the boys were given two. That bought a quart of *Old Dynamite.* Even with pulled punches, those oateater fight scenes were something to watch.

My favorite memory of Poverty Row was the weekend I spent watching a set decorator do over a period piece while the costume department whipped up a modern wardrobe for the heroine. In all the standing sets—bar, homestead, outside the general store, inside the general store, bright new signs were pasted advertising a popular brand of chewing gum. On Friday night the producer had pocketed a couple of grand from the gum company to change his picture from period to modern and show the hero opening sticks of gum at every opportunity.

This seldom happened on Poverty Row. Worse luck! Payola for the display of products was more common on the big lots. Indie producers survived by skimming their money off the top—grabbing the first thousand for themselves as salary and picking up whatever they could out of the budget in savings by chiseling on salaries, using stock footage, reverse chases, old sets—and automobile headlights.

Another Singin' Cowboy?

"DUKE" HAD A FAMILY TO SUPPORT, WHICH MEANT TAKING ANY ROLE AVAILABLE— EVEN THE PART OF "SINGIN' SANDY!"

Mr. and Mrs. John Wayne sun themselves at the El Mirador Plunge in Palm Springs in 1934. In the chair beyond Duke is actor Spencer Tracy.

Duke never worked for Harry Cohn again—even when it meant turning down *The Gunfighter* several years later, a classic Western directed by Henry King with Gregory Peck in the lead. Cohn, the eternal wheeler-dealer, assumed that money and a good script could *buy* John Wayne.

Not likely, for the Cohn indignities failed to stop after the completion of Duke's Columbia contract. They haunted him for quite some time afterward when he found himself bucking the worst innuendo an actor can suffer—rumors of unreliability.

Wayne made no secret of his fondness for booze. Those who knew him then—and later—respected his ability to hold it. Like any heavy drinker there were occasions when things got out of hand, but not many. Duke had too much respect for his work. He knew when to quit

if there was a morning call. Drinking never interfered with his work. He was always punctual and well prepared.

But after Cohn had ground him to the dust there was no place left for him to go but Poverty Row. True, Duke wouldn't have to hang around the Gulch, standing in line at the Cattle Call waiting for producers to come out of their store front offices to select riders and stunt men for a day's shooting. He did have an agent, a most respected one, Al Kingston.

True, Al didn't carry the clout of the big agencies but there was an advantage in dealing with him that a young fellow like Duke could appreciate. He was honest and when a client's back was to the wall, he knew how to bail him out.

Kingston negotiated a typical Poverty Row deal for Wayne, urging him to take it for the quick cash it would mean. A producer had acquired rights to some old Ken Maynard Westerns. They contained expensive production values, dramatic scenic backgrounds and plenty of hard riding. The producer wanted a new face to work in the closeups and fight scenes which he intended combining with the old Maynard footage. About four pictures were involved. It would entail fast work and give Wayne star billing and plenty of exposure to the Saturday matinee audiences. Kids didn't care whether a Western came from Metro-Goldwyn-Mayer or Monogram as long as the action played fast and furious.

Abruptly the producer balked. He'd gotten word that Duke was a drunk. It took Kingston a while to trace the rumor to Harry Cohn. The Poverty Row producer may have been at the end of the line of "Harry Cohn haters," but his dislike of the tyrant was strong enough to overcome his hesitation. Moreover, he knew that Cohn was fully capable of spreading a malicious lie. He signed Duke and he wasn't sorry.

In 1933 John Wayne married. His wife was Josephine Saenz, the daughter of the Panamanian Consul in Los Angeles. His first son, Michael, was born in 1934. Three more children were to come from his union with Josephine; Mary in 1936, who was nicknamed "Tony," Patrick in 1939, and Melinda who was born in 1940.

Duke wanted a large family although supporting a flock of children in the Depression took guts and plenty of hard work. Both qualities existed in John Wayne which explained not only how he agreed to work with Nat Levine but how he survived Nat and his bizarre world as *King of the Serials.*

Levine was a colorful Hollywood character, short, squat, ugly, with sharp eyes hiding behind thick lenses. He knew more about making movies than any man ever to hit Poverty Row. Any one of them would have made superb production bosses at the bigger plants if they possessed the imagination to understand the greatness of their medium. Virtually all the top assistant directors and production directors of the 50's and 60's were Poverty Row graduates.

Levine was so cheap that even penny-pinchers like the Alexanders loathed him. He went beyond the normal bounds of Poverty Row chiseling. An old-timer like Mr. Stern knew how many

telephone calls to make to get his kind of deal. After spending X number of nickels he was ready to compromise. Levine wouldn't. One of Wayne's recollections was working three weeks on a serial for a thousand dollars and starting a second one the following day to save the expense of returning the company from location. Levine worked his company eighteen hours a day, shooting exteriors in the sunlight; interiors at night. Directors like Breezy Eason, who knew their craft, stood still for the pummeling Levine handed them—there was no other place to go.

Levine carried no staff and planned no program for Mascot—even if he announced one grandly at the beginning of each selling year. This wasn't unusual. Even the majors made a big thing out of projecting a huge program of extravaganzas, half of which never reached the writing stage. So between serials, Duke worked where he could—grabbing stunt work if it came along, taking bits in pictures at First National and RKO.

Then along came Monogram, a shade better than most indies, because of its management; producer Trem Carr, for example. He was a soft spoken, quiet, dignified man with ambitions for Monogram that he knew could be fulfilled only if the company demonstrated a larger degree of integrity than his confreres along the Gulch. He signed Wayne for a series of Westerns, figuring his name was well enough known, his experience, excellent, his youth, a big advantage. Wayne was younger then the "old men" cowboys who were still holding on. Columbia had turned to young Charles Starrett to carry its Western program, and Carr believed Duke fitted into the trend away from the old-timers.

Carr had taste and class. Moreover he was an innovater. He'd toyed with the idea of a singing cowboy. Wayne shuddered but went along with it. The billing for his first picture read: John Wayne as Singin' Sandy in *Riders of Destiny.* But it wasn't Wayne's rumbling baritone that moviegoers really heard. Carr dubbed in the voice of Smith Bellew.

With Carr, Wayne enjoyed his first "feel" of stardom—even if his pictures were only five-reel Westerns. Wayne's background had prepared him unusually well to work with production. Carr respected his judgment. For the series they were able to attract above average writers and directors. The second lead was usually played by George Hayes who was equally at home as the heavy or comedy relief. Hayes, who came from burlesque, could perform with or without whiskers. Eventually, his white beard and skill at impersonating querulous old-timers earned him his nickname "Gabby" and many years of stardom with William Boyd in the *Hopalong Cassidy* series and later at Republic, where he performed as the sidekick of every sagebrush star who came to the Valley lot.

John Wayne winds up for a snowball fight with other members of the cast of "Shepherd of the Hills." Filming on location in the San Bernardino Mountains was temporarily halted by an unexpected blizzard. The picture was released in 1941.

Then there was Yakima Canutt, a legendary movie figure, who was usually cast as Wayne's chief antagonist. A warm relationship grew up between the two men and Canutt taught Duke many of the intricate tricks of stunt work.

Wayne began to develop his habit of dressing his characters away from the sterotype. The director wanted him in the usual white cowboy outfit but Wayne saw Sandy differently. He dressed him in a sweat-stained Stetson, a dirty old kerchief, a soiled checkered shirt, rumpled denim and worn boots. You could believe that Sandy had been on the trail for a long time.

Then Herbert Yates entered the scene. He was the owner of Consolidated Laboratories, a former Wall Street man, who had acquired the property through speculation and a simple curiosity and interest in the movie business. Yates longed to be a producer. Virtually every quickie producer in town was indebted to Consolidated, for the lab had first lien on every foot of film it processed. Yates may not have known much about movie making, but he knew everything about the bank accounts of the sharpies who produced them.

He formed a combine of Mascot, Monogram, a couple of others, and they all headed for the San Fernando Valley where Republic Pictures was started. A United Artists it didn't become. But Yates put money into the plant, built a fine Western street, added some sound stages and, as the producers gradually drifted away back to the States Rights field they understood better, Wayne became about the only property that had been part of the original Republic set-up.

Trem Carr slipped out to join Universal—and life for the next several years was as painful for Duke as it had ever been—if somewhat more rewarding financially. He was steeped in the Western rut.

At Republic Duke put down his guitar and Smith Bellew became his own man. Singin' Sandy was quietly retired and a new singing cowboy began to roam the range—Gene Autry.

Autry had a cherubic face that would have looked more comfortable behind a grocery counter; as an actor, he was ghastly; as a singer, only slightly better. But Autry had the Midas touch and gold poured into his ten gallon hat as though he had been its inventor. When Autry threatened to bolt Yates' stable, they created Roy Rogers, young, handsome, unaffected, very attractive. Roy became an instantaneous hit, so Republic had two big money makers going for it—and the Duke.

Roy must have borrowed one of Autry's hats, for riches began to fill his coffers as, like Autry, he spread his earnings around, investing in real estate, cattle ranches and things cowboys were presumed to know nothing about.

At Paramount another cowboy star was getting rich, William Boyd. The silver-haired veteran of the silent screen, a perennial in the films of Cecil B. DeMille, was hauled out of obscurity by producer Harry Sherman to play Hopalong Cassidy in that extraordinary series of Westerns.

It was Boyd who prevailed upon Sherman to film the series in color; Boyd who bought the TV rights and Boyd who made a fortune out of the whole *Hopalong* craze long after he'd been sidelined for the second time in his career. He had simply waited for television instead of fearing it as most Hollywoodites had in the years when its inevitability was predicted.

For two years Wayne rode through Western after Western for Herbert Yates and at the end of his contract he refused to renew despite unusually favorable terms. Instead he moved down the San Fernando Valley to Universal where Trem Carr had been installed as the producer of a series of action pictures. Both Carr and Wayne hoped they would lift him out of the cowboy class and bring him to a wider audience than the cowboy stars enjoyed.

It didn't quite work out as the old friends planned. Wayne played a variety of characters—a coast guard commander, a prize fighter, a trucker, a news photographer and a whaler. The Wayne action pictures were monumental failures.

Carr, the Poverty Row genius, had sold Universal the series on his promise to cut costs and bring them in on budgets similar to those he was accustomed to on Poverty Row. It didn't work out. It couldn't. At Lone Star actors would cut their prices for a week's work but not at Universal. In action pictures Carr couldn't use the stock footage that composed twenty-five percent of most cheapie Westerns. Carr's corner-cutting backfired. The series looked what it was—cheap. "We were trying to sell cotton hose in a silk stocking market," Wayne commented later.

With family obligations pressing him, Wayne went back to Republic, hat in hand, and accepted a deal to do the *Three Mesquiteers* series. He ignored John Ford's advice to limit the contract to two years, believing Herbert Yates' promise that if Duke agreed to a five year contract, he would play Sam Houston in a big special Republic had in the planning stage. When Republic eventually made the Houston film, Richard Dix played the title role. Wayne was told he wasn't "boxoffice."

It was a bitter period in Duke's career and there were times when he considered chucking acting and going in for something else—prizefighting, for example. He was over thirty, long past the age when the leading man pattern should have been established. He loathed the *Three Mesquiteer* series. They got none of the time and attention of the Autry musicals. The actors sometimes improvised their dialogue—but these films, more than any of his earlier work, gave Duke identification. He was teamed with Ray Corrigan, Robert Livingston and Mex Terhune, cool professionals, who did their jobs extremely well.

Duke remembered them with little affection, "Some of those Westerns I made were done in four days. I'd change my clothes, read the lines, change my clothes, read some more lines. We'd start before dawn, using flares to light close-ups. When the sun came up we'd do some medium-range shots. In full daylight we did the distance shots, following the sun up one side of the hill and down the other. It didn't matter who was the director. He had no chance, and I had no chance. They could still sell five reels of film with me riding a horse and that was that."

The *Mesquiteers* were a hit and the fans Duke had accumulated were delighted to find him back in the saddle where they could enjoy him as a Western hero, not as a boxer or photographer.

Wayne may have envied the bags of gold collected annually by Gene Autry and Roy Rogers (both men were extremely clever at business and land buying) but his own bag of gold lay only a few features away from the second series he performed for Republic, the Stony Brooke group. (Republic's films, westerns, hillbilly comedies, action pictures, etc. were done in "series" form.) Big Daddy had managed to sign him for the role of Ringo Kid in *Stagecoach,* a movie destined to become a landmark in movie history because it marked the greening of John Wayne—Superstar.

From the moment Wayne boarded the stagecoach to Lordsburg with passengers like Claire Trevor in "Stagecoach," his stardom was assured.

Stagecoach to Stardom

AS THE RINGO KID RODE INTO THE SUNSET, DUKE TUMBLED INTO A RAVINE OF GOLD!

Stagecoach first appeared in *Collier's* as a short story by Ernest Haycox, a master at the Western genre. It attracted John Ford's attention, then at one of several peaks in his career, and it hit him at the right time. Ford hadn't directed a Western in several years.

He bought screen rights to the story and brought the project to Walter Wanger, a pretentious Hollywood wheeler-dealer whom Ford could easily intimidate. Wanger, one of the few producers of the time who could claim a college degree, allowed no one to forget it as he rose from Paramount's eastern production office to a

producer's job at Paramount in Hollywood from which he moved to United Artists where he formed his own unit.

Wanger made Liz Taylor an instant millionaire as the producer who squandered *Cleopatra's* millions, who shot a rival in the groin after finding him in the company of his wife, Joan Bennett, and served several months at the Los Angeles County Honor Farm after pleading guilty to the assault. He was also the producer who did a stretch at Allied Artists when that company was a division of Monogram.

Thanks to the efforts of friends, still unidentified, he was able to accomplish a striking valedictory to his curious movie career when he filmed as his last picture *I Want To Live,* which won an Academy Award for Susan Hayward.

Wanger wore tweedy sports jackets, smoked a pipe, embraced liberal causes and disagreed with the Hollywood theory that "messages should be sent by Western Union."

Wanger felt incredibly bold when he filmed *Blockade,* which sided with the loyalists in the Spanish Civil War. It bombed. He attempted to reach great artistic heights with Ingrid Bergman as *Joan of Arc.* It lighted no fire at the box office. The public preferred *Salome—Where She Danced,* in which he starred Yvonne DeCarlo.

Wanger's successful production credits occurred when directors like John Ford handed *Stagecoach* to him on a silver platter or when terrible-tempered Fritz Lang barred him from the set while he was drawing an extraordinary performance from Henry Fonda in *You Only Live Once.*

Stagecoach was written for the screen by Dudley Nichols. The story brought six desperate characters together on a stage being driven to Lordsburg by a regular driver and a U.S. marshal. They stop to pick up Ringo Kid, an outlaw who has a rendezvous with the Plummer brothers for a showdown. Ringo's horse has gone lame, and the price of the ride is surrender to the marshal. When the coach is attacked by Indians, Ringo becomes vital to the rescue and, after he's settled his score with the Plummers, the marshall looks the other way, allowing Ringo to slip to freedom.

Ford lined up an impressive cast headed by Claire Trevor, Thomas Mitchell, John Carradine, George Bancroft and Andy Devine. He chose Monument Valley as the location and battled to cast Wayne as Ringo. The next step involved Wayne's persuading Herbert Yates to consent to the loanout. It took effort but eventually Wayne made his first giant step toward superstardom. No one ever imagined—perhaps John Ford saw it—how far Duke would travel after *Stagecoach.*

Tiresome Walter Wanger didn't, for he was the producer who had to be convinced that a B picture actor was up to the part—much less worthy of being in a Wanger picture.

Afterward, Wanger took credit for discovering Wayne, but that was to be expected. He also maintained that buying the Haycox story was his idea. Ford, however, kept Wanger at a safe distance. When the producer visited the location he was horrified to find Duke doing his own stunts—a part of the job that the actor took for granted.

One of Wayne's biographers, Maurice Zolotow, a skilled reporter, wrote that a souvenir program distributed at the Westwood theatre press preview

of *Stagecoach* contained such extravagant praise of Wanger's role in the production that a separate page had to be slipped inside it to acknowledge that such talents as Ford, Dudley Nichols and Ernest Haycox indeed existed. I was at the Westwood screening and can't recall the program, but that's a problem of memory. Hogging credit was the sort of thing Wanger was given to. Moreover, he believed what his publicists wrote about him.

Zolotow suggests that Wayne was disappointed by the equivocal notices *Stagecoach* and his own performance received from the *New York Times* and *Herald-Tribune*—as though equivocation were suddenly new to those papers. In its arts section (except for Ada Louise Huxtable's reports on architecture), *Times* critics still hem and haw—except that today their commentary

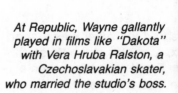

At Republic, Wayne gallantly played in films like "Dakota" with Vera Hruba Ralston, a Czechoslavakian skater, who married the studio's boss.

has grown longer, aimed largely at movie buffs who idolize obscure directors like Samuel Fuller and have memorized all the dialogue from *The Wizard of Oz.*

Yet, when Wayne faced the critics in *Red River* several years later, Bosley Crowther was hardly playing mumbledy-peg when he wrote in the *Times* that the many excellent performances were "topped off by a withering job of acting as a boss-wrangler done by Mr. Wayne. This consistently able portrayer of two-fisted, two-gunned outdoor men surpasses himself in this picture."

The main event of that night at the Westwood Village theatre appears to have been overlooked by historians—as well as the major protagonist—John Wayne. From the minute Duke appeared on the screen and steadily brought the Ringo Kid into focus there was absolutely no doubt that the audience was witnessing the birth of an important new star, a man in the same big league as Gary Cooper. If there were any references to his "oateater" background, they resolved themselves into wondering, "How is the poor sonuvabitch going to get out of Republic?"

Praise for the picture was universally enthusiastic; for a change Wanger didn't have to bribe reviewers. And Duke Wayne became the talk of the industry. For obvious reasons. He was the surprise. *Stagecoach* was a class Western, handsomely mounted, with an action-filled, suspenseful story, fascinating characters, a John Ford masterpiece. And what could one write that hadn't already been printed about Thomas Mitchell, Claire Trevor, Carradine and Donald Meek? Inevitably, Wayne grabbed all the space.

Bittersweet Success

DUKE LIVED THE AMERICAN DREAM
OPPOSITE LOVELIES LIKE MARLENE DIETRICH,
BUT THERE WERE NIGHTMARES TOO!

When Clark Gable was filming *Mogambo* in Africa it was his first encounter with John Ford, whose brusque manner of handling actors earned him a reputation as a tyrant. Ford was capable of reducing leading ladies to tears and driving tough actors to furies.

Gable asked for another take on a scene he felt hadn't gone well, an accommodation he was accustomed to. Ford cut Gable short and walked off the set without saying a word. Gable was furious and refused to speak to Ford for weeks afterward. Finally the producer, Sam Zimbalist, ended the feud. "Look, Clark," Zimbalist said, "Ford's used to John Wayne. When you get in there, just say, 'Yes, Coach' and you'll be all right." Eventually Gable came to admire Ford, but from a cautious distance.

For the first two weeks of *Stagecoach,* Ford pulled out all his nasty tricks to cajole Wayne into a performance that would achieve the level of the polished acting of the professionals surrounding him. On the third week, when Ford saw Wayne's strength emerging in the character of Ringo Kid, he relaxed.

Wayne's new career took off like a meteor— accomplished by the expertise, bargaining, wheeling and dealing, that Hollywood was capable of at that time. Almost overnight Duke was sur- rounded by a fresh set of "handlers." A major agent, Leo Morrison, bought Duke's contract, and rearranged his Republic deal so that Wayne became a free agent in return for doing a specific number of high budget pictures for his alma mater.

Republic promptly reissued Wayne's *Three Mesquiteers* pictures—to Duke's annoyance. Afterward, it was realized that they'd done him a great deal of good. Wayne was a new star in one area but, being an old face in quickie "horse operas," he was able to achieve instantly the heavy exposure that was the cornerstone of the star system.

Audiences suddenly discovered that Wayne was a cowboy star with sex appeal. No leading man could expect to become "boxoffice" without it. Wayne's sex appeal was conservative. Howard Hawks, who directed Duke in *Red River,* said, "In a love scene, Clark Gable always forced the issue. Wayne was better when the girl was forcing the issue." Said Vera Miles, "They used to say in the Old West, 'Men were men, and the women were

grateful.' Well, that's how Duke made you feel as a woman."

Wayne knocked off A pictures with the same speed that he filmed his horse operas. Wayne's first outside picture was *Allegheny Uprising* for RKO. His leading lady was Claire Trevor. According to gossip columnists, Claire and the screen's hottest tough guy were, in the language of their trade, a "hot item." Wayne hadn't been one of the stars newspapers wrote about. Little was known about his private life. At Republic, keeping his wife and children out of the limelight had not been a problem. Now it became difficult and Duke was troubled. He wasn't used to having his personal problems aired in public.

In many respects the Wayne marriage had been a happy one. There were the children, for one thing, to hold it together long after it had been a marriage in name only. There had been the sharing of hard times when Duke was a thousand dollar a picture serial star for Nat Levine, rising at four, getting home at midnight, spending weeks on location, jumping from one picture to another overnight.

It was a life Josephine hadn't been prepared for. She was a well educated, genteel young woman who felt uncomfortable with Duke's companions, his hard-drinking pals like Grant Withers and Ward Bond. She did move graciously in the quiet segments of Hollywood society. Josephine was a close friend of Loretta Young.

Duke's success, after years as a journeyman, was neither responsible for the disintegration of the marriage or for the failure of Duke and Josephine to give it a second chance. They had already gone the route, even to the point of consulting a marriage counselor.

But the differences between them were irreconcilable. But no one's interests would be served by making a break sooner than they did. They separated in 1942 and Josephine filed for divorce in 1944. It was uncontested and she was given custody of the children.

During *Allegheny Uprising* Duke got in the habit of not going home after work. The Hollywood Athletic Club saw a great deal more of him than in the days when he dropped by simply to work out before starting a picture. For as long as anyone could remember, the club had been host to unhappy husbands, ranging from top stars to new names like Wayne, so Duke, at least, lived in

John Wayne's success, after years as a journeyman, was bittersweet. His leading ladies, Marlene Dietrich especially, all warmed to Duke's charm and gallantry.

an understanding atmosphere.

When World War II broke out, Wayne tried to enlist but was rejected because of his age and family responsibilities. Like other stars in the same position, he contributed to the war effort by making appearances at hospitals and training camps. Wayne was enormously popular. He needed no props, no musicians, no pretty girls to ogle. Duke had only to be himself. The GI's identified easily with Duke. Having grown up with him through his Westerns, they regarded Duke as an old friend.

Like Humphrey Bogart, whose career took off when he was switched from heavies to romantic leads because of the wartime shortage of male actors, Wayne was able to jump from picture to picture, studio to studio. He also jumped off his horse and out of his Western clothes.

Duke didn't play many Western heroes in the forties. Instead he "won the war." At least that was the gag resulting from his work in *Back To Bataan, They Were Expendable, The Fighting Seabees.* He was nominated for an Academy Award for *Sands of Iwo Jima* which was filmed in 1949.

Duke may have been a bit unsteady out of the saddle, but there was conviction behind his "Let's get the Nips!" rallying cry.

Moreover, Duke personally welcomed the change of pace. He wasn't all that eager to be squeezed into the mold of the lean, lovably laconic man in the saddle. "Not that I had thoughts of becoming a song and dance man," he used to say, "but, like most young actors, I did want a variety of roles. I remember walking down the street one day, mumbling to myself about the way my movie career was going when I bumped into Will Rogers. 'What's the matter, Duke?' he asked, and I said that things weren't going so well. 'You working?' he asked and I said 'Yep.' 'Keep working, Duke,' he said and smiled and walked on."

Even if Will Rogers' advice was worth heeding, Duke was still given to sinking into the doldrums. "Once I was working a movie with Harry Carey and his wife, Olive, and I was complaining about being typed. 'Duke,' Ollie said, 'look at Harry over there—would you like to see Harry Carey play any other way?' 'Of course not,' I said. 'Well,' Ollie said, 'the American public doesn't want to see you any other way either. So wake up, Duke! Be what they want you to be ...'"

When he told that story, Duke got a mischievous smile on his face. "See," he said, "I'm not against Women's Lib. Ollie gave me some real good advice."

Harry Carey had been one of Wayne's idols when he was a kid. Carey had become a victim of Hollywood's vicious blacklisting of actors who wouldn't play the producers' game. He had starred in an MGM film, *Trader Horn*, filmed in Africa. A young girl, Edwina Booth, contracted a tropical disease on the location. She was a pretty blonde who played the feminine lead. The experience permanently damaged her health and led her into court with a suit against the studio. Carey refused to perjure himself by testifying that Edwina was ill before the picture began. In standing on his integrity, Carey kissed a flourishing career goodbye and had to wait for Duke to start him going again.

Duke had begun to discover the clout a movie star could exert. He enjoyed the respect shown him at the major studios and particularly the opportunity to create the Wayne image. He looked for simplicity, basic emotions, no particular nuance. In speaking of his Western roles, Wayne contrasted them with the vogue for psychological dramas. "There's no particular reason for a cowboy to go to the couch," he said. "He's not worried about what's going on in his head or whether the bastard next door is gonna steal his cattle."

In the glare of the spotlight, John Wayne emerged a far more complex and sophisticated personality than a cowboy star was supposed to be. Success uncovered a many-sided man who, having achieved the American dream, the success he had dreamed about, discovered that the "dream" could also be bittersweet.

In the years following *Stagecoach* he performed in a succession of films that satisfied the public's appetite for action but few tapped Duke's acting resources. The intense exposure John Wayne received during the war years and immediately afterward would bear fruit eventually but at the time the sort of film expected of Wayne set Duke to brooding that his work was not taken seriously. He murmured about the prejudices of the Eastern establishment critics. Wayne felt that his peers took him for granted.

Privately, Duke conceded that the break-up with Josie was difficult to accept. He didn't question its inevitability—he simply wondered— "How could this happen to me?" On the other hand, having watched the miserable experience of his parents in trying to hold together an acrimonious marriage, he knew that he'd chosen the lesser of two evils.

Duke was a born roisterer and in later years the days he recalled with childish pleasure were the hard-drinking sprees he's enjoyed with John Ford's stock company, Ward Bond, Victor McLaglen and the others. He could spill some fabulous yarns and the miracle was that the men survived some of their capers. Duke answered the unasked question, "Of course, you gotta remember that we were younger then."

Duke had never been a womanizer. There were girl friends at high school and college but Josephine was his first real love. Following his true blue American instincts, he married her. Without her and reduced to the role of a "visiting" father, Duke was lonely and uncomfortable.

In view of his heavy and continuous working schedule it was inevitable that there would be rumors about Duke and his leading ladies. Osa Massen, a pretty Danish actress, did not appear in *The Long Voyage Home*, but she'd been engaged to help him aquire a Swedish accent.

It could hardly have remained a strictly professional association. Miss Massen was not a teacher by profession but a well-respected artist. Her lessons with Duke took place at quiet restaurants and a warm friendship developed.

Osa was the first of a succession of foreign women who would figure in speculation about Wayne's private life. Sigrid Gurie, who appeared opposite Duke in *Three Faces West*, adored him and laughed at inquiries about the depth of her feelings by saying, "How could any woman not be charmed by John Wayne? It's impossible."

Sigrid probably was the first actress to give the Wayne off-screen image some definition. Duke was as old-fashioned and respectful of women away from the cameras as he was on the screen. His manners were impeccable; his politeness, awesome. He was a far cry from the traditional Hollywood "wolf" who needed to make every "broad" to reassure his masculinity, or the Hollywood "snake" who used the "I'll make you a star" approach and, failing that, would threaten reprisals. Ambitious young women ran a precarious obstacle course in the Hollywood of the *Golden Era*. Duke was popular because he was different. He even "listened."

Professionally, Duke was able to even some old scores. Cecil B. DeMille, who had been impressed by his recent work, wanted Wayne for *Reap the Wild Wind*. Years earlier, the mighty DeMille had snubbed Wayne. After receiving the script Duke returned it with a long list of suggested changes.

Wayne had been in the business long enough to realize that someone had to protect a star's image. The studios usually took care of it. Wayne eventually would chortle over the battles he undertook singlehanded to make sure the Duke got a fair share of the action. "Remember, I never had a big studio behind me. I had to look out for myself except, maybe, when John Ford would do it for me."

So his requests to DeMille were not totally born of pique. "I told DeMille that Paramount would take care of Ray Milland. I wanted to be sure I don't end up in a supporting role." His part was that of a skipper of a ship he purposely sinks in order to gain the salvage profits. It was a heavy and the character died at the end.

DeMille assured Wayne he'd not be slighted and the veteran producer was as good as his word. *Reap the Wild Wind* emerged as colorful, exciting DeMille, and as the crusty sea captain, Duke found the sort of part he could sink his teeth into.

Reap the Wild Wind was filmed in 1942, in the darkest days of America's wartime years. When colleagues came home on short leaves, Duke was visibly distressed. He suffered agonies over his inability to participate. Not until 1944 was he able to go overseas personally and extend the kind of relationship he'd made with the GI's on a one-to-one basis at home. When he came back, Wayne told Americans what was needed. "More letters, cigars, snapshots, needles and radios. They're fighting a helluva war. It's work and sweat. If it's one hundred and thirty degrees they call it a cool day. That's when they scrape the flies off."

Wayne played opposite virtually all the top leading ladies of the era, Joan Crawford, Claudette Colbert, Marlene Dietrich, Paulette Goddard, Susan Hayward and Jean Arthur. There were also some newcomers—Ella Raines, Donna Reed, Laraine Day.

For a time Duke was linked to Paulette, but it was the sultry Marlene who most fascinated him. They became close friends for three years during which they made a trio of pictures together— *Seven Sinners, The Spoilers* and *Pittsburgh*.

John Wayne was not the first of Marlene's Hollywood "conquests." She had been taking over Hollywood men ever since she landed Gary Cooper as her leading man in *Morocco*, Marlene's first English language picture. In *Morocco*, Dietrich was given reverse casting—a cabaret singer accustomed to exchanging her favors for

expensive baubles. Not so—not after she saw Gary as a French Foreign Legionaire. She taunted him with all the allure and sexual skills the censors would allow. Away from the set, where there were no censors, Marlene enchanted Coop. The affair set the pattern for all of Marlene's that followed.

"The moths hovering around the flame," of which she sang in *The Blue Angel*, hovered for indeterminate periods and then flew away. Marlene was married to Rudolph Siebert, the man nobody saw. But he was very much alive and real, even in the last decade of his life when he was confined to a sanitarium. Siebert served as an invisible presence which intentionally or unintentionally routed Marlene's lovers whenever she grew weary of them—or after they had tired of her.

Marlene's relationship with Duke was accomplished with more eclat and less notoriety than her liaison with Gary Cooper. Marlene was not nearly so possessive of Duke. She didn't have to be, for in Wayne she found a man whose interests matched hers to the tiniest detail.

Marlene was earthy, born to please men. She was a great cook, a marvelous housekeeper, knew old-fashioned remedies that cured everything from snake bite to hangovers; she liked the outdoors and didn't squirm at prize fights or balk at an invitation to a football game.

But the relationship of Marlene and Duke entered more dramatically into the private world of movie stars. To be a star one must love oneself and be totally committed to the profession. Marlene and Duke deeply loved themselves. They cared about their careers and to protect them they recognized the need to be masters of the medium. Marlene understood the technical side of movie making as well as Duke. Evenings when they might be expected to spend smooching were often devoted to watching and studying the films that circulated on the Bel Air circuit where Hollywood elite fought over the privilege of being the first to have a "private screening" of a hot new property.

When the war ended Marlene returned to Europe. She marched into Paris with the American troops. Duke, in Hollywood, was preoccupied with two important decisions, working out a new contract with Republic and Herbert Yates and deciding whether he would marry Esperanza Bauer, a sultry Mexican girl of twenty, who had done some parts in Mexican films. Her nickname was Chata, which translated into "Pugnose." She was beautiful, voluptuous, and married when she met Duke but in the process of a separation. Chata was strongly devoted to and influenced by her mother, whose maiden name, Ceballos, Chata used professionally.

The
Stormy
Years

FOLLOWING A TRAGIC MARRIAGE,
DUKE LOST HIMSELF IN WORK . . .

The end of World War II also spelled "finish" to the Hollywood the world knew as the fabled capital of the movie industry. When the big stars returned, it was not business as usual at the same old stand. Their hides had been toughened, their business acumen sharpened. There would be no more seven year "slave" contracts, suspension clauses and the numerous restrictions placed on their talents that existed before Pearl Harbor.

They wanted a piece of the action as well as the right to choose scripts, directors, co-stars, working hours—the lot. James Stewart was one of the first stars to finish up his old Metro-Goldwyn-Mayer contract in a hurry in order to step out and become his own man in the movie business.

By 1946 Wayne had a solid backlog of successful pictures behind him. The co-starring vehicles with Dietrich had been hugely successful; *Pittsburgh* was the only one of the trio that failed to hit big boxoffice gold. Wayne's named possessed real value at the boxoffice —even if he had not yet climbed to the ranks of the top ten. Audiences—critics especially—enjoyed the Dietrich-Wayne pictures.

Any major studio would have embraced John Wayne's independent unit, much as Universal accepted Jimmy Stewart's. Only Metro-Goldwyn-Mayer clung to the outmoded notion that it could survive in the tradition of the past.

Wayne chose to stick to Republic. Better a known devil than the unknown! He had tangled with Herbert Yates for so many years that it had become a habit. Perhaps he shared with Yates the dream that in the postwar years Republic might fulfill its "destiny" to become a major studio. Privately, Duke nurtured ambitions to direct. Possibly this was a reflection of his "graduate studies" with Marlene. Who knows?

Republic had done poorly by him in the pictures he'd done during his second contract,

signed in 1942. Morever, in 1945 he had been the "gallant" whose silence was never more eloquent than when he was asked about his relationship with Vera Hruba Ralston, a young blonde Czechoslavakian ice skater who, with her mother, had fled Czechoslavakia in 1938, finding refuge in England where she became an ice skating star. She added Ralston to her name and reached America as a star performer in the touring revue, *Ice Capades.*

Yates had bought *Ice Capades* for the screen, hopeful of turning Vera Hruba into another Sonja Henie. He was sixty-one at the time and absolutely crazy about the gorgeous young girl with the improbable name.

Ice Capades got a chilly reception at the boxoffice. Even chillier was the reception Vera Hruba Ralston received at the hands of the critics. Her Czech accent was impossible to penetrate; her acting, graceless. She was totally lost, however talented she might have been on skates.

She was a disaster compared to Sonja Henie, who was pert and saucy. Sonja was no great shakes as an actress either. But her diction was good and there was always a gleam in her eye that told the audience "not to worry," she didn't wear her ice skates to bed.

For all her beauty, Vera Hruba failed to convey basic elements of sex appeal. Nevertheless, Yates was determined to make her a star, and she was awarded to John Wayne as his leading lady in *Dakota.*

Dakota was a lighthearted piece in which Duke was pitted against Ward Bond, his old adversary, in a story about a land hungry enterpreneur who was trying to force farmers from their property by burning their crops. Yates cast Vera Hruba Ralston as his wife, inviting critics to suggest that Wayne had faced the "most challenging work of his career."

Today, in John Wayne television festivals, *Dakota, The Fighting Kentuckian, Tycoon,* in which he was again teamed with Vera Hruba, and *The Barbarian and The Geisha,* in which Duke portrayed Townsend Harris, head the list of films titled: *The Worst of John Wayne.*

But in 1945, who took Vera Hruba and Herbert Yates seriously? While they were filming *Dakota,* Duke's friends warned him whenever Yates was coming to the set—and Duke made it a point to be seen coming out of her dressing room, going into her dressing room, or loitering somewhere in the vicinity. Finally Yates put his own army of spies to work and the two co-stars were under constant surveillance.

What Yates couldn't believe was that Vera was irresistible and the last thing Duke's code of honor would consider was muscling in on the territory of his partner. He couldn't even bring himself to tell Yates the truth—that the affair was the laughing stock of the film colony.

One of the more unbelievable spectacles of Hollywood night life during the Yates-Ralston courtship was the sight of the old man on the dance floor of Mocambo and Ciro's whirling the lady around with *razzamataz* that Gene Kelly would have envied.

In later years, Duke never spoke uncharitably of Vera Hruba, saying only that she was inexperienced and that Yates showed poor judgment in letting his personal life intrude on business. That was later. If the truth were known, Wayne put up with Vera Hruba because he had his own personal "project" going and it would need the collaboration of Herbert Yates.

So Duke coached Vera Hruba in English by day; at night Herbert took her to the cabarets and when there was time, Duke and Yates worked out his new contract—both secretly hoping that this would open new horizons for Republic.

It didn't. The talent wasn't there—especially not at a time when stars were calling the shots—picking and choosing their deals with caution and an eye to the gross—not their guarantees and percentages. Republic didn't have enough clout to interest them. Herbert Yates, smart as he was, had gone as far as he ever would in the movie business.

Republic was never cut out to become a major in the sense of the movie business at the time—another MGM, 20th Century or Paramount. Republic eventually lost Autry and Rogers—and it would part company with Wayne even if Duke and Herbert Yates wrote a new contract which made him the first actor-producer since Charles Chaplin, the head of his own unit at Republic, yet free to accept assignments elsewhere.

But 1946 wasn't the year for the best intentioned movie men to work out partnerships. Old Hollywood and its world-wide monopoly on theatres, studios, talent, distribution, was under attack from all sides. The government had cut it down to size with a series of anti-trust suits that broke up the marriage of the studios and theatres.

In the face of the threat of television, Hollywood buried its head in the sand. Executives were shocked by the neo-realism of films like *Bicycle Thief* which came out of Italy before the dust of war had barely settled. "A kid pissing on the streets? My God!" They paid little attention to the fact that first the Italian government, then France and England, saw movies as a quick route to needed American dollars, so government subsidies turned film production in those countries from speculative enterprises to government-insured exports.

At home, postwar movie attendance dropped. The reasons lay beyond television and the dribble of European imports. Filmgoers had their fill of

Characteristically, Wayne fought the "runaway productions" of the 50's and 60's—films made abroad by Hollywood producers. Eventually Duke's own company joined the exodus.

the Hollywood style—lightweight comedies, the formula Western, the *Jones Family, Blondie,* musicals about Coney Island and Atlantic City.

Hollywood's postwar product survived because movie going was still the national habit. That changed when gasoline became plentiful, as new cars came off the asembly lines, bowling alleys opened up and other forms of entertainment drew on the strength of the movie dollar. Within four short years, some of the top talent in Hollywood would be working in Europe, representing a cross-section of the old movie colony.

They included Frank Sinatra, Cary Grant, Humphrey Bogart, David Niven, Robert Taylor, Kirk Douglas, Mario Lanza; actresses Ava Gardner, Audrey Hepburn, Katharine Hepburn, Claudette Colbert; producers and directors Robert Rossen, Stanley Kramer, Alfred Hitchcock; writers Irwin Shaw, Edward Anhalt, and virtually all the blacklisted survivors of the Hollywood Witch Hunt. Rome's Via Venta was nicknamed "The Beach," and they called Rome "Hollywood on the Tiber."

When the mighty Darryl Zanuck, production head of 20th Century-Fox, abandoned his studio job to head his own unit in Paris, there were harsh words between him and the Duke over what Hollywood called "runaway production."

Eventually Duke went to Ireland for *The Quiet Man,* to Libya for *Legend of the Lost* and seriously considered Peru for *The Alamo.* Even the Duke couldn't preserve Hollywood against the tide of changing tastes and the competition from foreign film makers.

World War II severely curtailed American travel habits. "Abroad" meant Canada or Mexico. Californians inevitably preferred Mexico and the frequent trips by the film colony there were not exactly frowned on by American intelligence agencies. A horde of Germans had come to America posing as refugees, only to slip away shortly before or directly after Pearl Harbor. Many were prominent in the arts. Visiting Hollywoodites to Mexico City were asked at the border to cultivate any of the refugees they came across in the hope that some might let slip valuable information.

At this point in his career Duke, looking for new horizons, was on extremely friendly terms with the top producers and money men of the business. He'd cultivated the press and the Wayne image had made its imprint on the average American, the guy who paid his money at the boxoffice. He was ready to hitch up his pants and move on to bigger achievements.

Among the powerful men who had noticed Duke was Howard Hughes who, after they became friends, often dropped in on him unexpectedly. "He was on the prowl for information about movies and movie making," was how Wayne explained it. "I thought Hughes knew all about it." Or, he might have been laying the groundwork for the deal Wayne would one day make at RKO after Hughes had taken over the studio.

In the forties, Wayne and a group of actors moved in and out of Mexico in search of a place to buy land and set up an independent film company. They frequently met Hughes during their visits. Mexico was a good drinking territory and a place to have fun.

On one trip to Mexico, Duke was obliged to attend a luncheon arranged in his honor by one of the studios outside Mexico City. The lovely girl sitting next to him was Esperanza Ceballos "Chata" Bauer.

She was an exotic—and Duke was attracted immediately. Chata was troubled with a skin problem which she made no effort to conceal. Wayne admired that. He also admired her perfect body, flashing teeth, Chata's wit, her readiness to laugh, and the way she handled her liquor, matching him drink for drink. He was told that Chata had played starring roles; she'd been particularly successful in a Spanish-language version of *The Count of Monte Cristo.*

Even if he wanted to, Duke couldn't possibly have shaken himself loose of his fascination with Chata—or her mother. She seemed the answer to his quest for someone who was the match of his lifestyle. Chata liked his friends, she was in the "industry," she understood the uncertainties of the profession. She laughed a lot. Chata was a good companion. Morever, Duke enjoyed the company of her mother who, like Chata, seemed the total professional.

One step led to another. Duke visited Chata in Mexico when he could. Telephone communication wasn't practical because of the War so Wayne wrote to her. He suggested a contract with Republic.

Chata accepted but not, as Duke hoped, at the suggestion of a contract. Chata knew how to play hard to get. It took time, so much time in fact that Duke became visibly upset by the girl's failure to respond. Finally, Howard Hughes flew Wayne down to Mexico to see her if, for no other reason, than to get Duke's mind back to Hughes' business—his desire to produce movies again.

Chata returned with Hughes and Wayne, tested for Republic, a formality, really. Yates was only too happy to give the young woman a contract, presuming that would settle whatever "monkey business" had been going on between Vera Hruba and Duke.

Chata never made a picture for Republic. She couldn't. Chata was too busy wrecking Duke's life and her own. After her mother had made several visits, Chata prevailed on Duke to allow her to stay with them. It wasn't comfortable. Wayne's house at the time was small; it amounted to small bachelor's quarters.

But Mother Bauer was happy because there would be no more separations from her daughter. Duke and Miss Bauer were married in January, 1946, with Ward Bond acting as best man.

What had been a stormy courtship became a stormier marriage.

It ended in bitterness in 1953 when Esperanza, with noted criminal lawyer Jerry Giesler as her attorney, went into court with a series of charges

John Wayne at the wedding of his
daughter Melinda Ann to Gregory Robert,
April 4, 1964

The Duke in a familiar scene while on location with "Sons of Katie Elder," 1965

John Wayne at the Playbill Restaurant to receive the 44th Annual Photoplay Magazine Gold Medal Award as "The All-Time Movie Box-Office Champ," March 3, 1966

John Wayne and his wife Pilar hold their daughter Marisa Carmela (born 2/22/66) shortly after her birth (3/12/66)

Duke and Maureen O'Hara, a favorite leading lady, during the filming of "Big Jake"

John Wayne and Kirk Douglas teamed for the first time in "The War Wagon," a 1967 movie

John Wayne being presented the Academy Award from Barbra Streisand for Best Actor in "True Grit" 4/7/1970

John Wayne at the Academy Awards, 1979

thing his money could buy.

In his face she flaunted her own unfaithfulness and the marriage deteriorated into one sullen day after the other, the atmosphere charged with hatred, alternating with moments of ecstasy. About a year after her return to Mexico, Esperanza had dissipated her annuity, moved into squalid quarters, turned her back on the world, drank tequila day after day. In the fall she was found in her dingy rooms—dead of a heart attack.

It was a sordid experience in Duke's life, and friends eventually pieced together the story of a man insanely in love with a woman who was enslaved by alcohol and dominated by an alcoholic mother who believed in corporal punishment. Mother Bauer had inflicted the beatings Duke was accused of.

Duke's illusions about Chata's character were shattered one by one. He expected to find in her a wife who would understand the nature of his work and forgive the irregularity of his hours, a woman who would try to make a home under conditions which would never be ideal. Esperanza simply lacked the capacity to understand what was expected. She resented sacrificing her own ambitions, which would have come to nothing under any circumstances. Duke, surrounded by drunks, had made the fatal mistake of marrying one.

As a sort of corollary to Duke's misfortune, there was the curious end to the reign of Herbert Yates as the Great Mogul of Republic. A group of stockholders led a revolt against the fortune Yates lavished on making Vera Hruba Ralston a film star.

Wayne privately complained that *The Fighting Kentuckian* suffered grievously because of Vera. It was a big-time picture, involving his own independent unit, but her ineptitude made it one of the few Wayne movies that lost money.

Yates solved the problem of the stockholders' revolt by marrying Vera. She retired from "acting." Yates died several years later and today the one-time Czechoslavakian ice-skater leads the genteel life of a rich widow amid the high society of Santa Barbara.

Duke had done a great deal for Republic. He'd brought John Ford in to direct *Rio Grande*. They had given Republic *The Quiet Man*. Other top directors began considering Republic as a respectable place to work—but it was too late. Too much damage had been done to his career to stick with a loser. Wayne decided it was time to strike out, keep his production company afloat and to distribute its pictures through the majors.

Howard Hughes would begin to take a prominent role in Wayne's fortunes, as would a lovely Peruvian girl he met while scouting locations there for *The Alamo*.

Until he moved to the major studios little was known of Duke's private life. When his second wife, Chata, charged that Duke beat her, his female fans raced to court with signs reading, "Duke, you can slug us around any time!"

against Wayne that described him as an inhuman monster. She complained of beatings, infidelity, drunkenness and on the stand seemed to relish recalling the intimate details of her life with Wayne. Because Wayne had successfully avoided scandal in his career, it smarted. It hurt to fight a woman. There was no alternative. Taking the stand in his own defense he denied the charges categorically and women outside the court carried signs saying, "Duke, you can clobber me any time."

Esperanza was granted a settlement of fifty thousand dollars a year for six years. She returned to Mexico—a shattered woman, victim of alcoholism, her unfulfilled ambition to become an actress, perhaps even disappointed at having failed at being a good wife to a man who had lavished on her things she never dreamed existed—beautiful homes, exciting trips, every-

A Voice From The Right

DURING THE COLD WAR, DUKE'S POLITICAL BELIEFS OVERSHADOWED HIS ACTING!

With fame there came change and a young man who one day was simply hustling bread for his wife and kids gradually became a complicated individual caught up in a super-active life that divided itself into three distinct and demanding parts: his professional world as an actor-producer, his private life and Duke's curious role as a political spokesman for Hollywood's conservative wing, considered by its opponents—and victims—as reactionary.

That Duke chose conservatism as his political philosophy was curious; that this genial, easy-going graduate of Poverty Row, who enjoyed a rowdy night out on the town with his buddies, who was worshipped by his family and friends as "the finest" would take on the headaches of politicking seemed totally out of character. Like many young men who became of voting age in the Depression, he had been a Roosevelt Democrat.

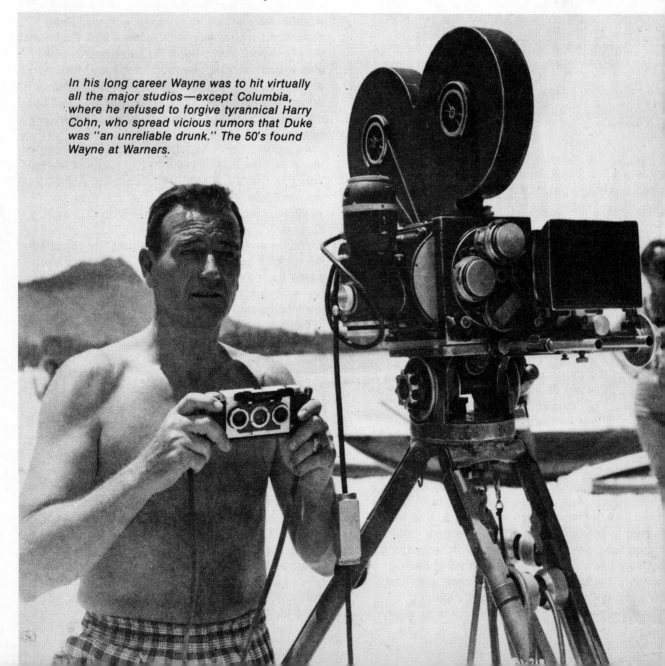

In his long career Wayne was to hit virtually all the major studios—except Columbia, where he refused to forgive tyrannical Harry Cohn, who spread vicious rumors that Duke was "an unreliable drunk." The 50's found Wayne at Warners.

In 1944, there came the organization of the Motion Picture Alliance for the Preservation of American Ideals. Its first public meeting was held at the Beverly Wilshire Hotel, attended by about fifteen hundred persons, representing the craft unions and a group of top stars that included Gary Cooper, Irene Dunne, Barbara Stanwyck, Ginger Rogers, Ward Bond, Clark Gable, Robert Montgomery and Adolphe Menjou. Other notables were musical director Dimitri Tiomkin, producers William Goetz, Cecil B. DeMille, Mike Frankovitch; directors Norman Taurog, Sam Wood, Victor Fleming, John Ford. The lone studio head present was Walt Disney.

A far less impressive group of screen writers was composed of Borden Chase, James Edward Grant, James Kevin McGuinness (who also produced), Emmett Rogers, Morris Ryskind and others.

The writers, however, were the powers behind the formation of the Alliance, the fellows who wrote the speeches, made policy and did the thinking. They were the right wingers who had suffered a crushing defeat in the organization of the Screen Writers Guild and its recognition as an instrument for collective bargaining with the studios. They had lost out in writing the Guild's constitution and in fielding their slate of officers—defeated by a militant, vocal, labor-minded group of liberals.

The question reporters should have asked was, "Who paid the rent for the Beverly Wilshire grand ballroom that night?" and much more would have been understood about the Alliance.

Adolphe Menjou's presence was obvious. The excellent actor, noted for his sophisticated roles and fabled wardrobe, had become fanatical on the subject of Communism. He had been making lists of subversives for years, listing suspect barbers and waiters at posh restaurants whose accents were suspicious. The Alliance could use Menjou either as house goat or effective speaker.

Sam Wood, Norman Taurog and Victor Fleming enjoyed close ties with Metro-Goldwyn-Mayer, Wood and Fleming were under contract. So was Robert Taylor willing to show up where the studio wanted him.

With so much MGM present, the Alliance

Until the 40's Wayne had paid little attention to politics. Then he became concerned with the so-called "Commies" who were "infiltrating" Hollywood. He joined the notorious Motion Picture Alliance for the Preservation of American Ideals, whose Red baiting wrote an ugly chapter in Hollywood's history.

origins would have to tunnel back to Louis B. Mayer, the "great tycoon" who cherished political string pulling as much as persuading stars like Jeanette MacDonald and Milija Korjus to sit on his lap while they signed their contracts. His was a bottomless purse, implemented by his control of a stable of stars, brainwashed to participate in his politics.

Director Sam Wood was elected president of the Alliance and it was agreed that regular meetings would be held thereafter. At first, the Alliance caused little stir, having been formed at a time when groups proliferated in such numbers that it was virtually impossible to keep track of them.

Political activists were not new to show business, and when you dug up their roots they led to the labor struggle. Producers battled unionization; they paid tribute to Al Capone's goons as the price of labor peace and rigged elections to place company stooges into office in independent unions.

The genesis of the Alliance was the liberal victory in the Screen Writers Guild. That had been the last straw and it was interpreted by the losers as symptomatic of a *malaise* embracing all the professional guilds. They decided that a small group of Communists, under party discipline, would take over the unions and control American movies. The first meetings were held at the home of James Kevin McGuinness. Wayne attended one of these informal discussions, brought by old friend Ward Bond. He said nothing but listened as McGuinness, Sam Wood and others discussed the Communist dangers existing in Hollywood. Wayne was concerned by the writers' warning of a "Commie takeover of the Screen Writers Guild."

In 1969, Duke told *Time Magazine:* "There's a lot of yella bastards in this country who would like to call patriotism 'old-fashioned.' With all that leftist activity I was quite obviously on the other side. I was invited to a couple of cell meetings, and I played the lamb to listen to 'em for a while. The only guy that ever fooled me was the director Edward Dmytryk. I made a picture with him called *Back to Bataan*. He started talking about the masses, and as soon as he started using that word—which is from their book—not ours—I knew he was a Commie."

(Dmytryk, called before the House Un-American Activities, at first took the Fifth Amendment. He admitted later that he had been a Communist between 1944 and 1945 and had undergone a change of heart. When Dmytryk returned to directing, he hired Adolphe Menjou. Asked how he could possibly work for a Communist—even a "rehabilitated Red," Menjou replied, "Because I'm a whore.")

The Alliance and the House Un-American Activities Committee cast twin specters of fear

over Hollywood. On his side of the fence, Duke claims that anyone affiliated with the Alliance was branded an anti-Semite, a Nazi and, in his case, a lout, drunk, clown and faithless husband. It was maintained that until the Alliance came into existence, known conservatives like Adolphe Menjou had suffered blacklisting, along with writers like Jim McGuinness. Pat O'Brien blamed his affiliation for difficulty in finding roles as a freelance actor.

Clark Gable succeeded Sam Wood as president of the Alliance, to be followed by Robert Taylor. In 1948, Wayne became president. According to Maurice Zolotow, Wayne supported a resolution by Roy Brewer that "Los Angeles, with the second largest representation of Communists in America, should register all Communists."

There were the absurdities, yes, that made the Alliance ridiculous. And there were the laughs in Washington when the Un-American Activities Committee asked Lionel Stander if he had ever attended Communist cell meetings, "Sure," he said. Asked why, the gravel-voiced comedian answered, "To meet girls."

Others could not be so flip. Some went to jail for contempt of Congress—for refusing to identify themselves as Communists, a legal

Gary Cooper and Duke at a SHARE benefit.
The foundation raises funds for mentally
retarded children. Duke's contribution to the
entertainment consisted of singing "Home
On The Range" to the highest bidder.

Although Wayne deplored the shift of film
production from once glamorous Hollywood
in the 1950's, he was compelled to join the
flight and himself become a "runaway
producer." Here he's seen at a London
press conference.

political party in all forty-eight states. The point of
confrontation between the Congressional
Committee and those summoned for hearings
was the right of the individual to keep his political
affiliations private, personal and secret. For the
witnesses to have identified themselves as
Communists, assuming some were, exposed them
to naming others. Or incriminating themselves if
Congress suddenly decided that, like the
Japanese-Americans, Communists represented a
danger and threat to the country's security.

It was tricky debating, hence the lawyers for the
Hollywood victims chose the Fifth Amendment as
the logical route of defense. This invited a charge
of contempt of Congress and possible prison, a
penalty not generally associated with political
activity in the United States.

Yet Chairman Martin Dies brandished his whip
and talented men were jailed: Dalton Trumbo,
Ring Lardner, Jr., Adrian Scott, John Howard
Lawson, all brilliant writers, producers and
directors. Dmytryk was among them but, as has
been noted, he recanted.

There were those who were simply labeled
"unfriendly witnesses" when they refused to
answer the so-called $64 Question, "Are you now
or have you ever been a member of the

Wayne actively campaigned for Ronald
Reagon. Fellow supporters of the B picture
actor turned politician were Bob Hope,
Dean Martin and Frank Sinatra.

Communist Party?" They automatically suffered
the blacklist; brilliant careers were snuffed out
overnight, among them, Academy Award winner
Gale Sondergaard, Anne Revere, J. Edward
Bromberg, Will Geer, Larry Parks—so many
others.

There was the tragedy of John Garfield—he
was on all the lists, but the Committee never
subpoenaed him. Finally, long after the hue and
cry had died down, he appeared as a "voluntary,
friendly witness" and proclaimed his patriotism,
insisting he had never been a Party member. It
was a lonely decision—and it came too late. His
career had already been wrecked; alcoholism did
the rest. Garfield died prematurely at thirty-nine of
a heart attack. Carl Foreman, the author and
co-producer of *High Noon,* fled to Europe, as did
Sidney Buchman, a distinguished intellectual,
who had produced the two *Al Jolson* pictures.

The cruelty of the Alliance, the self-serving
publicity the Un-American Activities Committee
generated for itself—the obvious tricks were not
appreciated by the public at large. Older
filmgoers, remembering the Great Depression,
could understand how young actors had been
lured into Communist membership.

Although the American Legion heads constantly
threatened "picket" and "boycott" of movies
employing "Commie Rats" there was no
groundswell of support from rank and file
members. The Witch Hunt produced no uproar for
the heads of the personalities named as Reds.
The public didn't give a damn. The Alliance was

recognized for what it was—an illegal vigilante
group.

Inevitably rifts developed among the
anti-Communists. Duke, for example, felt that
those who recanted and cooperated with the
Un-American Activities Committee should be
forgiven and past sins forgotten. However, when
Duke praised Larry Parks for admitting his leftist
associations, he incurred the wrath of Hedda
Hopper who wrote:

"I was shocked as I read the statement of our
president John Wayne, which would imply that he
voiced the opinion of our Alliance. If it did—we
should so express ourselves. It is not my opinion.
I wish to be personal from now on.

"I too have sympathy for anyone who sees the
light, but Mr. and Mrs. Larry Parks were visited by
a member of the FBI four years ago—who
pleaded with them to give up their membership in
ths Communist Party. If they had listened, Larry
Parks' appearance in Washington would not have
been necessary . . ."

Eventually the Alliance was shamed out of
existence, and the Un-American Activities
Committee, after years of idleness, was quietly
retired. What had all the hysteria of those years,
the accusations, the counter-accusations
produced? No bombs were found in the garages
of the men who went to prison nor in the
apartments of the ladies who had been drummed
out of Hollywood. No subersive movies were
uncovered although, according to Robert Taylor
in his Congressional testimony, MGM was guilty
of a "naughty" when at the request of the State
Department, it made a boxoffice bomb, *The Song
of Russia.*

But interest in the era of the Red Witch Hunt
has awakened the curiosity of historians, who
have begun to sift the records with care. They
have discovered that innuendo was preferred to

facts, flag-waving substituted for documentation, that little kids were barred from working in the movies and on TV because their mothers and fathers had attended rallies of organizations sponsored by Governor and Mrs. Herbert Lehman, Eleanor Roosevelt and the Honorable Fiorello LaGuardia, Mayor of the City of New York.

Afterward, Duke became active in the Republican party, supporting Goldwater, Nixon and, for a time, defending Spiro Agnew until the full import of his misconduct in office had been revealed. Duke became an articulate Vietnam hawk; in 1968 he opened the Republican National Convention in Miami with an inspirational address.

Of the early members of the Alliance, some have gone on to that great Beverly Wilshire ballroom in the sky; others are seldom heard from—certainly not in the context of their work with the Alliance. Only Wayne was still active enough politically to have been at the end of a rumor in 1972 that he had been selected as George Wallace's running mate for the presidency. Duke answered "bullshit" and the papers, taking him at his word, printed DUKE SAYS B———T TO WALLACE RUMORS.

With the years attitudes softened and it was clear that Duke eventually felt uncomfortable when reminded of the days of the Motion Picture Alliance. Zolotow reported a little-known fact involving *True Grit*. After accepting the lead, he got a telephone call saying that the author, Marguerite Roberts, had attended meetings of the

Wayne was the kind of actor who "had trunk—would travel" for any good cause. This was taken at the Cotton Bowl in Dallas when he spoke during "Action Now," a drug abuse rally.

Communist faction in the Screen Writers' Guild twenty years previously.

"Wayne blew his stack," wrote Zolotow. "He told the informant, in a blaze of profanity, that he did not care what Miss Roberts had done years before, but that the script was a fine script, and it expressed American principles, and he did not give a damn what a person had once been or once done."

To say that John Wayne shook the Conservatives was putting it mildly when he endorsed the Panama Canal Treaty in the face of pressure from old friends like Barry Goldwater to lend his voice to the opposition. On viewing that dreadful mass suicide at Guyana, Wayne felt that this was an example of brainwashing that ordinary people could finally understand. He joined in the movement to free Patty Hearst by saying, "If one man can brainwash nine hundred people, imagine what brainwashing did to one little girl—Patty Hearst."

In one of her books Hedda Hopper wrote that the day after Duke joined the Motion Picture Alliance, he was warned by an important producer, "You've got to get out of that MPA. It will kill you at the boxoffice. You'll hit the skids." According to Hopper, Duke commented about his work with the group, "I hit the skids all right. When I became president of the MPA in 1948, I was thirty-third in the ratings of boxoffice leaders. A year later I *skidded* right up to first place."

Duke was oversimplifying, of course. He explained his own popularity more incisively when he said, "It's very simple. I never do anything that makes any guy sit out there in the audience and feel uncomfortable. So when the little woman says, 'Let's go to a show,' the guy says, 'Let's see the John Wayne picture,' because he knows I won't humiliate him. I think the guys want the girls in."

Most of the millions of people who attended Duke's movies had probably never heard of the MPA. Even such an anti-establishmentarian as Steve McQueen was a Wayne fan. "Sometimes kids asked me what a pro was," he said, "I just pointed to the Duke."

Terry Robbins, a Chicago coordinator for the radical S.D.S. at the time he was asked about Wayne, said, "I consider Wayne terrific and total. He's tough, down to earth, and he says and acts what he believes. He's completely straight and really groovy. If they wanted to really make a movie about Che Guevara, they ought to have Wayne play him." Abbie Hoffman volunteered, "I like Wayne's wholesomeness, his style. As for his politics, well . . ."

When asked in his last years if he had gone a bit soft on the Bolshies, Duke thought a while and answered, "Communism is quite obviously still a

Wayne was an enthusiastic gun collector, although he admitted being a "lousy shot." Mexican authorities recovered a portion of his extensive collection, which had been stolen from his Newport Beach home.

Bob Hope professed to be apolitical for many years, but his gradual drift to the conservative wing of American politics lost him many fans. Wayne, on the other hand, thrived on the controversy over his politics. He enjoyed satirizing himself. In this TV special he played a conservative father; Hope was his hippie son-in-law.

threat. Yes, they are human beings, with a right to their point of view . . . but you certainly don't want your children to share their point of view. That's all I'm interested in—seeing that they don't disrupt what we've proven for two hundred years to be a pretty workable system, a system in which human beings can get along and thrive."

Writer P.F. Fluge was enthralled by an afternoon with Wayne who roamed critically,

John Wayne was awarded the Americanism
Gold Medal Award at the 1971 convention of
the Veterans of Foreign Wars. Commander
Herbert Rainwater made the presentation.

sometimes angrily, over a wide variety of
subjects—Dr. Spock, Vietnam, the impossibility of
changing things in America, his distress with the
State Department, the United Nations, welfare and
minorities.

Wrote Fluge, "If you wait long enough, John
Wayne will say all the things we have learned to
expect him to say, not to win fans or gain votes,
but because they really trouble him. But as we

listen to him the voice fades; the louder he talks,
the less it matters. When we remember him, we
will not see an aging movie cowboy pacing in
anger by a swimming pool at the edge of the
Pacific. We will see him when he was a younger
hero, on horseback, in the Monument Valley of
thirty years ago. We will picture him a proud
figure in a bright and clear landscape which
recedes away from us—and from him."

The Duke Becomes King!

AFTER 21 YEARS ON THE SCREEN, DUKE FINALLY BECAME THE WORLD'S NO. 1 BOX-OFFICE ATTRACTION!

In 1947 when Wayne was forty he appeared to
be losing his strength at the boxoffice. There
were reasons; his new pictures at Republic had
been only average and in his zeal to keep working
as an antidote to his personal problems Duke, like
Willie Sutton, went where the money was, to the
bigger studios where he was slugged with trivia
like *Tycoon* and *Angel and the Badman*. These
were made at RKO where he'd finally been lured
by Howard Hughes.

In 1948, he was thirty-third in the *Motion
Picture Herald's* annual evaluation of boxoffice
stars. Their calculations were reached by careful
polling of theatre owners. Thirty-third would have
delighted any number of stars with their names
over the title but not Duke.

It depressed him and as he often did
throughout his career, he mumbled about the
tough row he'd hoed for himself. Duke
complained that everything he'd achieved of value
had been accomplished on his own or in
collaboration with friends like directors Ford and

In his marriage to Pilar Palette, Duke seemed finally to have found a beautiful, sensible and intelligent wife. The Peruvian actress gave up her career to become a wife and mother. The youngster is daughter Aissa.

Henry Hathaway. He regretted having cast his lot—against everyone's advice—with Herbert Yates. To sour him even further, Howard Hughes hadn't represented much of an improvement.

Duke had come into the business at a time when a star's career was believed to be the equivalent of a dog's age—seven years. If one counted *Stagecoach* as the point where it all began for Duke, he'd been a star for a decade. According to the rules he might as well forget the rest of his life as a topliner, start playing character parts, turn to directing or settle down and beat the bushes for financing to produce his dream—*The Alamo.*

Then, there came *Red River.* It was filmed in 1948, but it didn't reach the screen until 1950. In the meantime Duke had done *Three Godfathers* with John Ford at Metro-Goldwyn-Mayer, *Wake of the Red Witch,* one of Duke's better Republic pictures and *She Wore A Yellow Ribbon* with Ford directing.

Wayne's performance in *Three Godfathers* as one of three bank robbers who find and protect a child as they flee across the desert was hailed as one of his best. In Ford's direction, the old Peter B. Kyne comedy-drama held up exceedingly well and the film was a hit. In *She Wore A Yellow Ribbon,* Wayne played a Union officer ordered to destroy the home of his Southern wife; an act leading to a long estrangement and separation

from his son. It had been a James Warner Bellah *Saturday Evening Post* story and, like most of Bellah's writing, it adapted brilliantly to the screen.

Wayne, having saddled up again, rode into 1949 in fourth place in the Motion Picture Herald poll, right at the top with Bing Crosby, Bob Hope and Abbott and Costello.

With the release of *Red River* in 1950 he became Number One. From this exalted position, Duke ruled for year after year, sometimes dropping back to second place when colleagues like Gary Cooper, who also began topping the poll as a mature star, temporarily borrowed the crown.

Wayne set a record of twenty-three appearances in the top five of the poll—a reign that topped Clark Gable's and left Cooper's dragging. "Coop" made the top division sixteen times.

Two factors played into Wayne's sudden break out of the corral. He played older men, tough guy roles, yes, but they were laced with compassion. Duke's audience always identified with the characters he played. In *Yellow Ribbon* and *Red River* they emphathized with more sensitivity than before. In *Red River* Duke worked with director Howard Hawks who was molded in the John Ford school. He was strong-willed, fiercely independent and, like Ford, enjoyed a strong attraction to the

Duke was proud of the second family Pilar helped create for him, happy in the home life that had been missing in his earlier marriages.

Western as exciting pictorial terrain against which one could weave outsized dramatic situations, yet reduce them to ordinary conflicts between human beings.

Red River was a romanticized version of the founding of the famous King Ranch in Texas, centering around a massive cattle drive over the Chisholm Trail, past the Red River and into Kansas City's market. Its principals were Thomas Dunson, a rancher with no respect for the law as he forces animals and men across the prairie through grim determination, and his son, Garth, sensitive but, like his father, strong-willed. The conflict arises from Garth's disgust at his father's tyranny which leads him to take control of the herd at the risk of murder by his own father.

Hawks was a "star maker," one of those rare theatrical talents who enjoyed discovering new talent (Lauren Bacall) or giving a new dimension to a familiar name (Carole Lombard, whose career had been undistinguished until Hawks cast her opposite John Barrymore in the bawdy comedy, *Twentieth Century*).

Hawks had noticed the work of Montgomery Clift on the stage and considered him ideal for Garth, providing the actor could reach the inner strength he needed to sustain the physical and emotional conflict with an actor of Wayne's power.

Clift admired Wayne and sensed the challenge playing opposite him would offer. Encouraged by Hawks, Monty learned to ride within a month. By the time production was ready to start, the actor, five feet ten, slender as a reed, had mastered all the physical requirements of the part. He'd become a first rate cowpoke and at the end of the picture Hawks presented him with an old five-star Texan hat that once belonged to Gary Cooper.

Duke was wary of stage actors as a matter of principal. He was even more wary of *young* stage actors, especially those who had been touched by *The Method* or insisted on working out every detail of a character so far in advance that on the screen no spontaneity was visible. When Duke met Clift he asked Hawks, "How in tarnation do you expect him to stand up against me in all those fight scenes? How's it going to be worked?"

Hawks confessed he didn't know himself. He reassured Wayne that a half dozen other young actors were standing in the wings ready to take over if Clift didn't work out. That mollified the veteran. After all, he had survived Vera Hruba Ralston!

In Robert LaGuardia's *Monty,* an excellent biography of Montgomery Clift, the author recalled the details of the first confrontation between the two men. Wrote LaGuardia, "The sequence had Monty stand by smoldering quietly, while Wayne ordered the execution of some of his men trying to desert. Monty told Hawks before the scene that he would play every line resolutely, to convince the audience he was a match for Wayne, but Hawks said, 'No, don't try to get hard, because you'll be nothing compared to Wayne. Start by taking a cup of coffee and watch him all over.' Monty understood . . . underplay the first part of the scene, throw the lines away as if there were something far more important going on in his mind. The effect was electric. Wayne, always quick to admit that he was wrong, went over to Hawks and said, 'Any doubts I had about that fella are gone. He's going to be okay!' The rushes that night showed Wayne's determination perfectly matched by Monty's eyes, and cool, suppressed time-bomb manner. Monty's character had been established.''

Having achieved the pinnacle, becoming Hollywood's top box-office star and with the agony of his marriage to Chata behind him, Duke plunged into his work with renewed fervor, now more than ever before, determined to fulfill his ambition of filming the drama of *The Alamo*. To Duke it was more than a movie; it would represent the sum total of his life's work. He would later say of *The Alamo*, "We wanted to create a moment of history that will show this generation of Americans what their country stands for.''

But *The Alamo* persisted in remaining a nagging dream as offers called him from MGM in Culver City to Warner Brothers in Burbank. Besides, there was his own company Batjac for which Wayne did several pictures.

Duke's marriages had been costly and while he was not given to a grandiose life style, Duke had an affinity for sidelines. He invested heavily and some of his risks eventually paid off. But he was in the position of many businesses which go through long spells when their cash flow hovers between zero and double zero. Duke needed to work, yet when television was a reality and he could name his own figure for anything he chose to do—specials, series, whatever—he declined. They offered him *Gunsmoke*. "I prefer the big screen," he explained. Although he turned it down he recommended that the producers have a look at a young fellow he knew, Jim Arness. Later, Duke would laugh and say, "Jim's got more money in the bank right now than I ever had in all these years of working." Duke was right.

On the set, Duke was the dedicated craftsman. He was the joy of directors, those who knew him and those working with him for the first time.

Sheilah Graham once wrote:

"Duke is not always good-tempered. He can look angry when actors are not on time. When he glowers, you must watch out. That is when he is ready to lash out. His language can be pretty strong, but he won't swear when women are around and he won't play a scene if he has to hit

Duke, Aissa and Pilar at home. The Duke finally settled at Newport Beach, where his boat was moored. He also maintained a ranch in Texas.

Pilar took her responsibilities as Duke's wife seriously. There were spats, of course, but they always made up before their "mystery separation."

Once Duke began topping the list as the world's Number One Boxoffice Star he seldom strayed out of the top five. Pilar and his family made these the happiest years in Duke's life.

The Hawaii location was fun for Aissa, who tried her talents as a hula dancer aboard sightseeing boat as proud Duke looks on.

The kids went traveling with Duke. Here is Aissa with Dad on location in Hawaii where he filmed "In Harm's Way," and squared off against terrible-tempered director Otto Preminger. Both survived.

a woman (you can't count the spanking he gave Maureen O'Hara in *The Quiet Man).* When Kirk Douglas was late one morning, Wayne said sarcastically, 'Well, we're waiting for our star. He's ruining our happy atmosphere.' Then he stomped off, talking under his breath.

"He is bossy on the set. He will tell people who argue with him, 'Shut your mouth.' During *The Sands of Iwo Jima* he explained to one of the other actors how he should have done the scene. He was interrupted by Robert Dwan, who said, 'I'm the director and I like the way he did it.' Wayne pouted but did not walk off. He is always early, always knows his lines and everyone else's. He is good to the crew and loyal to the actors who work for him.

"Wayne is a definite man. He is the kind of optimist who would have driven west in a wagon. He feels his presence is necessary on the set as a morale builder whether he is in the scene or not. He was not in the opening action of *The Hellfighters,* but he stayed until twelve-thirty the first night and the next until four in the morning. He was on his feet, never resting, chewing tobacco filched from the stuntman. When I asked him, 'Why did you want to do this picture?' (about oil-well fighters), he deadpanned, 'Oh, about a million dollars.' "

Duke was a realist; he'd spoken his piece about "runaway production—films that were taken out of Hollywood to shoot abroad where costs were lower, labor cheaper." He could not buck the tide and even his beloved *Alamo* was once involved in a production plan that might take it away from the United States.

He visited Peru in 1953 where the landscape, similar to Texas, might serve as background for a portion of the production. The expedition did nothing to further *The Alamo* but it did provide the meeting place of Duke and his third wife, Pilar Palette, a young actress, just twenty-four.

Once again Duke had been smitten by a Latin girl—this one, bright, vivacious, energetic, with a lot of common sense in her young head. There was so much common sense that she didn't even pretend that meeting *Numero Uno* in the movie world was the event of her life. She liked Duke,

enjoyed meeting him and their dates together proved pleasurable.

But when they met again—Pilar had come to Hollywood to finish some work on a picture—it was a different story. She fell in love with the rugged, handsome, blue-eyed actor. After a whirlwind courtship, they were married on November 1, 1954. The marriage produced three children, Aissa, John Ethan and Marissa.

Pilar was quite a change from Duke's previous wives, a cool young woman who, having been a professional, took the Wayne life style for what it was. There were no hopes for changing it, and

why? She got along well with Duke's friends; she enjoyed location, and the Wayne buddies basked in the warmth of her charm and genuine affection for them. It was remarkable how well she fitted into things.

Not that there weren't rough storms now and then—life with Duke had turbulence written into it—but for once Duke found a woman whose strength matched his, a woman capable of being just as blunt, direct and honest. So instead of quarrels becoming the end of the world, they became reasons for making up and renewing an affection that appeared to deepen with the years.

The luckiest break of Duke's life was having Pilar at his side when he was hit with the Big C—and if you want to include a professional note—to enjoy the comfort of his quiet moments with her when he was being slaughtered for *The Green Berets* and *The Alamo*.

The Alamo came first in 1960, and among the trivia reported as the expensive fiasco began was that Duke wouldn't hear of portable septic-tank johns when the huge company set up location on a ranch of several hundred acres outside of Brackettville, Texas, close to the Mexican border. Five miles of piping were laid to facilitate the installation of modern plumbing that flushed.

In the movie circles of London and Rome, where Duke's name provoked shudders, that must have come as quite a surprise to the Italian and British crew who had the misfortune to work the Libyan location of *Legend of the Lost* in 1958, a Batjac production, produced by Duke and director Henry Hathaway. Sophia Loren and Rossano Brazzi were the co-stars, making it eligible for Italian government subsidy and status as a co-production.

All the preliminary work, the selection of the location at Ghadames, an oasis situated at the center of an ancient camel route leading to Tripoli and the sea, had been organized by Duke's production crew. If they consulted either the Italians or Libyans they employed to assist in the preparation of the production, there were no signs of it. The whole affair was a mess, from start to finish, an American-made mess.

I was on location with Duke and the *Legend of the Lost* company and, for all his charm, unfailing politeness, Duke, I discovered, had an edginess about him that was anything but attractive in a man his size and importance. The Duke had his failings and they seemed enlarged, I guess, because of who he was.

We expect too much of heroes. Like most newspapermen who'd covered his long career, I might have disagreed with his politics but I couldn't fault his loyalty to his friends, his extraordinary generosity. His politeness and manners, I sometimes thought, belonged to another generation. Stars didn't often come through to jaded reporters with Duke's sincerity. You believed him because *he* believed in what he was saying. There was no questioning the man's integrity.

But he was not above moodiness. When I knew him better in 1957 I saw flaws in his character that were perfectly natural but they became magnified because they didn't belong with the tall, confident Wayne image.

He was fifty and, in many long, private conversations we had, he appeared to be childishly eager to turn back the clock. He would look at photographs of himself and mutter, "If I were only twenty years younger, the things I'd like to do." He mumbled—not too loud—that the photographers were taking too many pictures of Sophia Loren. "After all, who's the star here?" he asked.

I managed to get Sophia to pose with the Tuaregs and their camels, not an easy accomplishment. The veiled Arabians were superstitious about being photographed at close range. I couldn't hold them long enough to get a picture with Duke. He was furious.

It was petty. It was out of character.

Eventually I understood that Duke possessed that amazing capacity to separate his real personality from his screen image. If Wayne sometimes looked petty, he actually was watching out for the best interest of Wayne, the star.

Anyhow, you could forgive him most anything when the chips were down. Wayne, more than any celebrity I ever met, knew all his faults, admitted them freely; recognized when he was wrong and never felt awkward about admitting it.

Duke, Hathaway and the American crew organized the desert location as if it had been put together by Nat Levine for one of his serials. Although Europe is famed from the Baltic to the Mediterranean for its camping equipment, Batjac Productions shipped a boat load of surplus Army junk from Hollywood to Genoa, thence to Tripoli where a tent city was built—resembling the Hoovervilles of the Depression. The tents were shabby, stained, full of holes. The septic toilets were too small and too few. Once they were installed the showers functioned erratically leaving half a dozen soap-covered men to make out as best they could until water pressure resumed—sometimes, the following day.

Batjac had shipped the kind of food that suited the particular tastes of the Americans—hundreds of cans of pork and beans, cases of pickled onions, corned beef, corned beef hash, canned potatoes, canned tomatoes, tons of pancake mix and cans of maple syrup, corn flakes, canned corn. And canned American coffee.

The Arabs refused to eat the canned stuff, fearing it might contain pork. Italians loathe corn and demanded *pasta*. No one wanted anything to do with pickled onions or the corned beef hash. And everyone, including Americans who worked abroad, despised American coffee which lost its famous reputation during World War II.

There was a threat of a strike unless more suitable food was provided and camp conditions improved. Duke and his men couldn't understand the resentment. Weren't the Americans feeding and housing underprivileged Arabs, Italians and English?

A new cooking staff was installed.

On location, miles away from the camp site, I found Sophia Loren crying. No toilet facility had been provided in her dressing room trailer—nor for the other women on the set, Sophia's

At 56, when he was again voted the world's most popular movie star, Duke told London newsmen, "The older I get the more popular I become."

hairdresser and the script girl. Duke's men were surly when told of this—as they were about everything involving relations between the Americans and the Italians and Arabs. The last two were always referred to as "they" as were Sophia and the two women. "Why can't *they* use the sand—like the rest of us?" was the answer. An accommodation, however, was made the next day.

Wayne was surprised by the reaction to his tent city—and to the complaints of the "foreign" crew. In his mind's eye he was giving them a break—work, three meals a day and they were beefing? The American attitude of Duke's "boys" was characteristic hard-hat, "Well, if *they* don't like it, why don't *they* go home? Who needs *them?*" No one considered that they were employing skilled studio technicians, most of them capable in French, English, their own language, of course, and even, some Arabic. They had grace and manners—besides being tough, hard-working men, every inch the match of the Hollywood craftsmen.

The response of Duke and Hathaway to every mishap was petulant and snarling. Everyone was stupid—except themselves.

You had the feeling that Wayne, obsessed with his "tough" image, expected the same from everyone else—that, for a few bucks a week, everyone was supposed to be "tough" too. And if you didn't like it—there was always Russia.

Yep, there was always Russia. And England too, for when Duke badly needed a helicopter to get some aerial shots of the Tuaregs riding across the desert astride their camels in their blue veils—one of the great visual scenes in the picture—even super-American Duke Wayne couldn't wheedle a helicopter out of Wheeler Air Base.

The U.S. brass there claimed it would be flying outside their range of control for helicopters! But the British came through. They cheerily provided a chopper, a pilot to operate it—and no one at Whitehall seemed disturbed. The British blokes, a mere handful compared to the hundreds of Americans at Wheeler, came to watch the shooting, and it turned into quite a jolly day—and evening. One of the few pleasant memories *Legend of the Lost* left behind in the Libyan desert.

Perhaps, remembering that winter of discontent of *Legend of the Lost,* Duke had profited from the experience and was determined not to repeat his old mistakes in filming *The Alamo.*

Battling the "Big C"

DUKE DEFIED HOLLYWOOD TRADITION
BY TALKING ABOUT HIS CANCER OPERATION
AND BY URGING OTHERS TO HAVE CHECK-UPS!

Duke's dream *The Alamo* found its way to the screen in 1960. Like John Wayne, the film was larger than life and controversial, creating a brouhaha that touched the presidential campaign of that year, the Academy Award nominations, Duke's personal and professional relationships as well as his fortune and his health. Its complexities move *The Alamo* to a position in this narrative where the effect of the picture can be assessed as a total experience; hence the account of that curious venture appears later.

In achieving *The Alamo,* Duke fought the hardest battle of his career; but when you saw the Big Fellow on television in a public service appearance for the American Cancer Society, the Duke was talking about a far greater battle—his fight for life. He spoke candidly as an old, trusted friend whom we had known for over thirty years. Because of the kind of pictures he made, Duke knew us too. He had seldom disappointed his audience nor, as he so often said, "made anyone feel uncomfortable." His frankness about cancer made no one uncomfortable—only thoughtful.

So we listened when Duke said, "It happened in real life. I was just finishing my ninety-ninth ridin', jumpin', fightin', picture. Never felt better in my life.

"But my family nagged me into getting a medical checkup. And it turned out I had lung cancer. If I'd waited a few more weeks I'd be kicking up the daisies now.

"So friends, I know what I'm talking about when I tell you, get a checkup. Talk someone you like into getting a checkup. Nag someone you love into getting a checkup.

"And when the lady from the American Cancer Society rings your doorbell, dig deep in your pocket. They're working to rid this world of cancer once and for all."

The Alamo was far from a world-beater financially. Duke, who had invested a large part of his personal fortune in it and borrowed heavily from banks, immediately set out to repair his financial situation. There was only one route open—working harder than ever—as if that were really possible! Duke always worked hard. Jumping from picture to picture had become his way of life. This time, however, he accepted deals like a five picture commitment to Paramount at less than his usual money. He also did cameos in *The Greatest Story Ever Told* and in *The Longest Day,* Darryl Zanuck's vivid drama of D-Day, the massive invasion of Europe by Allied Forces.

Duke played Lieutenant Colonel Benjamin Vanderhoot, who led a battalion of paratroopers on a descent into Normandy. Although other cameo players in the all-star cast accepted roles for twenty-five thousand dollars or so, Wayne held Zanuck up for two hundred fifty thousand because of an old antagonism born of statements Zanuck once made about actors meddling in production and contributing to the decline of the movie industry by making excessive demands.

Of the cameos Wayne played at this time the most significant was that of General Randolph in the true story of Colonel "Mickey" Marcus who helped train the Israeli army. Wayne's appearances in *Cast A Giant Shadow* had an interesting background. The idea for the picture originated with Melville Shavelson, one of Hollywood's top comedy writers. He was captured

Duke and Pilar had reason to smile! Duke lost no time in returning to the limelight after winning his battle against the Big C.

by the idea of dramatizing the story of Colonel David Marcus, the American Jew who licked the Israeli army into shape to face the threat of Arab attack at the end of the British Mandate.

Kirk Douglas came forward to play the role of Marcus but Shavelson found himself up against a stone wall when it came to obtaining financing. Having been turned down by numerous Jewish production companies he got the idea of tackling Wayne for one of the cameo roles. No one, he reasoned, could accuse Wayne of being pro-Israel, but there was a point to the story that agreed with Duke's hawk-like attitude toward Vietnam—the idea of the United States becoming involved in another country's affairs. Wayne's interest helped generate the financing. Frank Sinatra also played a part in the ambitious drama which, unfortunately, turned out neither the artistic nor the boxoffice success promised by the story.

In 1963 for the first time in his life Duke felt poorly. He's been smoking five packages of cigarettes a day for years. He was able to consume an almost incredible amount of alcohol daily without affecting his conscientious work habits. Illness had never held up a John Wayne movie.

Pilar persuaded him to consult a doctor. He drove to La Jolla for his yearly examination at Scripps Clinic. An X-ray plate showed a spot on his lung. At Scripps they told him to enter the Good Samaritan Hospital in Los Angeles where the spot was diagnosed as cancer. Duke was told he would lose a lung.

Because so much rides on a star's health— insurance, contracts, commitments— secrecy is the standard operating procedure when someone of Duke's importance was hospitalized. Hollywood seethed with rumors and his representatives sought to calm the press with noncommittal statements. Eventually reporters got at the truth and Duke, characteristically, began taking the press—and his fans—into his confidence.

Duke laid it right on the line to writer George Carpazi:

"It was a rough operation. They had to take out the top of my lung and I lost a rib. Then they found that they had to yank me open again for edema after I swelled up like a puppy—it was the fluid collecting in my lung. But I licked cancer—the Big C as they call it. I caught it early. I was lucky. I hope my story will get other people out for checkups with the docs so that some poor soul can be as lucky as I was. I lived to tell the tale and now I'd like it to do some good.

"I don't want to turn people's insides when I'm talking about it, but I've got to level with my fans. I don't want anybody to feel having cancer is like having leprosy. This is something you can talk

After waging the fight of his life, with Pilar constantly at his side, the Waynes separated. The reasons behind their estrangement were never made clear. Pilar, who gave Duke a second family of three children, remained close to Duke's compound at Newport Beach in California. She told newsmen who inquired about the separation, "I talk to Duke every day on the telephone. He seems to prefer the company of his secretary."

about—and something you can beat. I beat it—because they found it early enough.

"After they operated on me and took that thing from my lung, it looked like everything was going to be all right. But in any operation there's always the danger of complication—and it happened to me. While I was in the intensive care unit I began coughing. I coughed so much that I busted some tissue, and that's when I developed the edema—the abscess which caused an abnormal

John Ethan Wayne, eight, gets a big hug from his dad, John Wayne, after they finished shooting a scene in "Big Jake." It was John Ethan's first featured role. The boy had been an extra with his father in "Rio Lobo."

amount of fluid to accumulate in my lung.

"It was then that the doc said I'd have to be operated on again.

"They put me back in the intensive care unit.

"My physical condition improved rapidly. My appetite was great, and they were letting me get a crack at some man-sized meals like soup, steaks, pork chops, salad and all the trimmings. That, of course, was after I came off the intravenous feeding. It got so that the nurses would needle

In his later years, Duke finally found time to enjoy his family. John Ethan and Dad take the famous stagecoach ride at Knott's Berry Farm and Ghost Town in Buena Park, California.

Duke and son John Ethan at Knott's Berry Farm in Buena Park, California.

Because so much rides on the health of a movie star, Duke's illness at first was kept a secret. Eventually Duke took his fans into his confidence, telling them that by catching the disease early, he'd been able to regain his health. Wife Pilar's strong support gave him the emotional strength he needed.

Patrick Wayne, 31, was also prominent in the cast of "Big Jake." In this scene he's treated to the kind of licking Duke dished out to the "bad guys" year after year in the 200 or more pictures he made.

me about my appetite.

"I was moved into a private room where I could watch television.

"I caught Jackie Gleason's show but he drove me nuts. I watched him lighting those cigarettes, and I'd have to look away. I guess I don't have to tell you that smoking was out for me. And I was a five-pack-a-day smoker. For forty years I smoked five packs a day—and the unfiltered kind.

"That was my only discomfort—not being able

John Wayne and son Patrick at the presentation of the Scopus Award, given by the American Friends of the Hebrew University at the Century Plaza Hotel in Los Angeles.

to drag on those cigarettes. But I've begun getting used to being a non-smoker.

"I don't go by the Hollywood code that cancer or some other serious illness can destroy a box-office image. And I don't buy what my advisers said—that the public doesn't want its movie heroes associated with cancer.

"What I say is the public—my fans—want the truth. I say there's a lot better image when John Wayne *licks* cancer."

For Duke, winning the Oscar was the fulfillment of a thirty year-old dream! Barbra Streisand opened the envelope that named him Best Actor for his performance of "Rooster" Cogburn in "True Grit."

Finally! The Oscar!

JOHN WAYNE'S PERFORMANCE IN 'TRUE GRIT' BROUGHT HIM HOLLYWOOD'S HIGHEST HONOR!

No wagon train ever led Westward Ho! by John Wayne met more disasters, dust storms, Indian raids, bad guys and good guys than Duke's quest for the biggest trophy of them all—the Oscar. He'd won all the others, most popular star, boxoffice champion, enough honorary police badges to decorate an apartment building, scrolls rewarding his charity work, letters of appreciation from cities, states and governments applauding his character, Americanism, humanitarianism and all his other sterling qualities.

But Duke had to toil long and hard as an actor before the moment arrived when he could stand up and race down the aisle at the sound of the magic words, "The winner is . . ."

It wasn't Duke's performances that got muddled in the playoffs; first, there was the vulgar pandering for votes by his publicists; then there was Wayne himself. If he alienated whole groups of people, from Hollywood colleagues to ethnic minorities, with his position on sociological and political problems, he became his own worst enemy when it came to Hollywood's annual Academy Awards. For starters, there was Duke's most frequently heard complaint, "If they'd vote

for the performance instead of *against* my politics, maybe I'd stand a chance."

Duke might have been right but he could also have been wrong. True, the Academy Awards *fiesta* involves partisianship, studio pressure, personal popularity and even vendettas but, by and large, the winners have earned their crowns. Some, for the wrong picture; others, because they were fresh, new faces; many, because their career achievements deserved it.

Duke first came up for a nomination with *Sands of Iwo Jima;* he was among the candidates for nomination for *Shepherd of the Hills.* He thought he was nominated for *She Wore A Yellow Ribbon*—at least that's what he told one interviewer. To another, he mentioned, "I shoulda been up for *Yellow Ribbon.*"

Any actor who has appeared in nearly two hundred pictures didn't have to apologize for getting his nominations and non-nominations mixed up. But Duke generally was either flustered or furious when it came to the most sensitive areas of his career; the Oscar, his mistaken belief that Hollywood took him for granted, his conviction that "intellectuals, radicals and method people" in the profession loathed him because of his outspoken conservatism and that the Eastern critics, the "elitists" of the newspaper profession, had written him off years earlier as no more than a stumblebum cowboy actor who had wandered into A movies by accident.

Nothing could be further from the truth. Legend has it that Wayne started to simmer when the *New Yorker* magazine brushed off his work as the

Duke put on an eye patch to portray "Rooster" Cogburn in "True Grit." Here he's seen with leading lady Kim Darby, relaxing on the set.

Ringo Kid in *Stagecoach.* Duke, until then, read, enjoyed and respected the magazine. As presidents have been known to react to newspapers they considered "unfriendly," Duke crossed the *New Yorker* off his subscription list.

He got upset when reviewers called his performances "typical Wayne" or if they wrote that "Duke, as always, played himself." He used to say, "It seems nobody remembers how different the fellows were in *The Quiet Man, Iwo*

Jima or *Yellow Ribbon,* when I was thirty-five playing a man of sixty-five. To stay a star you have to bring along some of your personality. Thousands of good actors can carry a scene, but a star has to carry the scene and still, without intruding, allow some of his character into it.''

Here Duke made sense instead of parroting his friend, Spiro Agnew, who did not enrich his short and shabby political career with his remarks about the Eastern Establishment. It remained very much in business, having sturdily survived the barbs of public figures who mistakenly assumed that divisiveness was the key to saluting Middle America. They insulted Middle America's sense of proportion.

Duke Wayne could never have run the thousands of cattle along the range of a hundred odd Westerns if the Eastern Establishment wasn't there to buy them. No man who had been before the public for nearly fifty years, thirty-five as a major star, had much to complain about. He'd been paid handsomely, been honored by his peers, adored by millions of fans and accorded the respect his talents deserved. Becoming a querulous old man, sniveling about Establishment newspapers, ill suited the tall-in-the-saddle image Wayne spent a lifetime creating. But pettiness was an old Wayne character defect. As friends grudgingly admitted, ''Duke could be awfully small time.''

Skip a couple of decades between *Iwo Jima* and *The Alamo* and we meet the Duke producing, directing and playing the lead in a filmnization of the heroic defense of a crumbling Texas fortress in 1836 against overwhelming Mexican opposition. It represented one of the most glorious episodes in American history. Wayne's writers had not exaggerated when, as the opening titles put it, the battle of the Alamo represented a moment when Americans had to choose between accepting oppression and making a stand for liberty. Historically, the defeat of the Alamo contained the seeds of victory; the men who died there gained valuable time for the Americans to consolidate their forces and overthrow the dictator Santa Anna at San Jacinto a few weeks later.

Again and again Wayne had promised to make *The Alamo* and to film it as an accurate historical document. It had already been worked over by Hollywood in quickie productions but that didn't seem to bother Wayne. It shouldn't have. An *Alamo* by Wayne held great promise but few people saw it from Duke's point of view—not Herbert Yates for whom he'd done so much—nor Howard Hughes who slugged Duke with the most lethal blow of his career by asking Wayne to put on an Oriental moustache and in the title role of *The Conqueror* cut an absurd-looking figure as the twelfth century Mongol leader, Temujin. Duke

and Susan Hayward, who played a beautiful Tartar captive, shuddered at the mention of the film.

Both Yates and Hughes refused to back it. It was brushed off at Warners, where Wayne turned out a series of pictures in the second half of the fifties. United Artists ultimately ponied up the financing for the first six million dollars. After that Duke was on his own. To complete *The Alamo* he mortgaged his production company and whatever else he could lay his hands on. Aside from corporate funds, Duke put a million dollars of his own on the line.

Wayne played Davy Crockett, and that was the beginning of the carping. He was obviously too old. If one listened to Duke's buddies, *The Alamo* was doomed before it started. They insisted that a conspiracy existed to blast Wayne's testament to his Americanism by beginning the nit picking the day Duke started directing. When John Ford

arranged special screenings for Academy members. There was heavy advertising in the trade papers. In February, 1961, *The Alamo* won a Best Picture nomination; Chill Wills was nominated for Best Supporting Actor, Dimitri Tiomkin for his score, and William Clothier for the photography.

Hollywoodites maintained that it was a shoo-in for *The Alamo*. Beside it, the competition was weak: *Elmer Gantry, The Apartment, Sons and Lovers* and *The Sundowners*. Chill Wills, a B picture Walter Brennan, could have won on sentiment. Dimitri was an old campaigner in the Academy sweepstakes and Clothier looked a cinch for the cinematography Oscar.

Russell Birdwell, a colorful press agent of a more naive era, the tub-thumper who maneuvered the search for Scarlett O'Hara onto the front pages of the nation's newspapers, created a tasteless campaign suggesting that a vote for *The Alamo* affirmed one's faith in the United States. Then Chill Wills took out an embarrassing series of advertisements in the trade papers. One listed the stars with whom he'd worked. Another contained the names of famous Texans who urged Wills' election. In a third advertisement, borrowing from Mike Todd who graciously thanked the members of the Motion Picture Academy of Arts and Sciences by listing their name *after* he'd swept the Oscar derby with *Around the World in Eighty Days,* Wills did the same, adding his own message: *Win, Lose or Draw, You're still my cousins and I love you all.*

An annoyed Groucho Marx took out a full page ad and it said: *Dear Mr. Wills, I am delighted to be your cousin, but I am voting for Sal Mineo.*

The episodes of bad taste did not stop with the Wills advertisements, but the end appeared in sight when on arriving in Los Angeles from London, Duke was asked how *The Alamo* stood in the Oscar race.

Wayne said grimly: "This is not the first time *The Alamo* has been the underdog. We need defenders just as they did one hundred twenty-five years ago this month."

The slogan making the rounds of the Academy voters was: *Forget The Alamo.*

They did. *The Alamo* and all its contenders were defeated.

The Apartment won Best Picture.

Skip another nine years when the embarrass-

visited the company for a few days, the scuttlebutt ran that he'd taken over. When it was finished, United Artists cut fifty-two minutes out of the print, eliminating key scenes.

However, the presumption that *The Alamo* was a total flop was incorrect. Yes, Wayne could say, "See, I told you so" when the "elitist" Eastern critics knocked it. Still it was reviewed seriously; critics were careful to give Wayne credit for his direction, particularly his handling of the action scenes. The production was praised, the brilliance of the camera work, noted. The screenplay was found flawed, and it was.

Wayne movies had survived bad reviews before. What happened to *The Alamo?* At the end of 1960 *The Alamo* was in the running for nomination in the Best Picture category. A nomination could add a million to the picture's gross; a win would mean several millions. Wayne's press agents

ments of *The Alamo* were buried in the past and admiration for Duke's personal courage had been an inspiration to everyone who knew him, either intimately or from his years as the guy who could lick anything. He'd bounced back from his bout with cancer as feisty as ever and was soon busy at his job. Pilar complained that she had to make appointments to even kiss her husband.

In 1968, Hollywood newsmen found Wayne where he belonged—"out" on location, disinclined to reminisce about the past. He was all fired up by his role of Rooster Cogburn in *True Grit.* Wayne had read the Charles Portis novel and knew that the character of Rooster would give him the best character he'd had in years. He tried to buy the property but producer Hal Wallis had beaten him to it.

It was just as well, for in Wallis, The Duke enjoyed a skillful producer with experience as extensive as his. It wouldn't be amateur night and to have produced *True Grit* himself would have been to invite a responsibility Wayne really didn't need at this stage of his life.

"Rooster was the kind of marshal the screen had never seen," Wayne said. "An old, sloppy-looking, hard-drinking, disreputable man who'd been around long enough to realize you don't mess with outlaws. You just use all the tricks in the book to bring 'em to justice—fair or foul."

Portis obviously had written the novel with Wayne in mind. This wasn't the clean-fighting hero of the sagebrush of his early career but a portrait of what happened to a marshal who had seen it all. Rooster's values hadn't changed. Just his style. He still believed in justice. But he dealt with it differently. He'd realized that in dealing with outlaws a kick in the face was clean fighting. Rooster brought his prisoners back alive—unless they got obstreperous. Then he killed them and slung them over the backside of his horse.

Wayne's performance as Rooster climaxed his fairly conventional work in the sixties which had included his controversial production, *The Green Berets.*

Morale builders were badly needed in Vietnam. Duke had barely recovered from his cancer operation when he volunteered to go to Southeast Asia. He used the same technique that served him in World War II, a monologue that moved casually into a conversation with the soldiers.

The result of that front-line encounter with dispirited Americans involved in a war they couldn't understand was *The Green Berets.* Duke came back feeling he had to tell the story— although, like Goldwater, he believed the whole Vietnam business could be disposed of by massive bombings of the enemy, even if it involved atomic force.

Wayne dragged himself through the production of *The Green Berets,* playing a role poorly suited to his age. But the picture needed the quality he would bring it. It was propaganda pure and simple—the only movie made glorifying the Vietnam War. Duke was alone. He stood on his convictions. He made the film against everyone's advice.

Unfavorable reaction had to be expected under the circumstances, and criticism went far beyond the circle of the Eastern Establishment. The reviews were brutal in New York, and they were brutal elsewhere. New Yorkers didn't bother to picket *The Green Berets*—but they did elsewhere—even in Middle America.

John Wayne had taken the second and the most unnecessary beating of his professional career. But this time he showed more maturity and settled matters by confining retaliatory statements to simple declarative sentences. "I felt the movie needed to be done. I still think it's a damned fine show."

When Duke was nominated as Best Actor for *True Grit,* there was none of the hoopla that accompanied the announcement of contenders for honors in the year of *The Alamo.* Duke allowed that he wouldn't mind winning the Oscar. "Just put down that I have plenty of room on my mantel for the award."

This time around there were no complaints about elitist reviewers, the radical left or the supportive right. Asked why he hadn't won an Academy Award before, he said thoughtfully, "Well, my career was mainly tied up with medium-priced productions. Most Oscars go to the lavish pictures, the big movies."

It was a time to mend fences as well as Wayne's attitude toward the Eastern critics. In studies of Wayne's career, biographers again and again quoted the big magazines, the New York *Times* and the arty publications. One seldom encountered clippings from papers West of the Rockies. Of Wayne's performance as Rooster Cogburn, William Wolf wrote in New York's *Cue Magazine,* "When the John Wayne retrospects are in full swing, this will loom as one of his finest movie triumphs. Wayne steals the film."

The public agreed and so did the voters of the Academy. Wayne won over tough competition from John Voight and Dustin Hoffman for *Midnight Cowboy,* Richard Burton in *Anne of the Thousand Days* and Peter O'Toole's *Goodbye, Mr. Chips.*

When Barbra Streisand opened the envelope and announced that the winner was John Wayne, Duke ambled up to the stage and made his speech. It was quiet, there was no flag-waving and it ended with, "If I'd known what I know now, I'd have put that patch on my eyes thirty-five years ago."

Duke had finally filled out his mantlepiece.

While his son clutches the famed statuette, John Wayne receives congratulations of friends at the Academy Award ceremonies.

A Living Legend . . .

HE SURVIVED ALL THE BATTLES AND WON A PLACE IN OUR HEARTS FOREVER . . .

Emotionally, the sixties had drained Duke. They'd been difficult financially, involving him in that enormous workload to pay off his personal obligations on *The Alamo.* When he was asked if he felt that the monstrous appeal to patriotism to sell the picture had affected its success, Duke answered crisply, "It didn't help."

In spite of the universal disapproval of *The Green Berets* it had turned into a money-maker, so Duke, who had produced it on his own, was not burdened with the added responsibility of paying for his stubbornness in tackling an unpopular subject.

He had finally landed his Oscar, but it was a bittersweet triumph. His mother, Mary, had died at the age of eighty-three, just before the Awards ceremony. Missing that night were John Ford and the members of the "Ford Stock Company"—Ward Bond, Victor McLaglen, Grant Withers, James Edward Grant, who had written so many of Duke's screenplays, and a half dozen others. Gary Cooper was dead; so were Humphrey Bogart and Clark Gable. Of the stars who could truly be called "giants," only Duke remained.

Was there another mountain left for him to climb—another stream to be forded—another cavalry march to be led?

You bet there was. Wayne had lived long enough to see himself a *Living Legend.* He had no intention of disappointing his fans. The lines were clearly drawn. Everyone knew and understood the Wayne image. Over the years it gained respect; it won admiration from the "arty" directors like Jean Luc-Goddard, who once asked himself how he could "hate" John Wayne's support of Goldwater and love him tenderly when he abruptly takes Natalie Wood into his arms in the next-to-last reel of *The Searchers.*

Wayne's image on the screen was attractive

In the last decade of his life John Wayne had become a Living Legend—a giant of the screen whose fine performances in "True Grit" and "Chisum" were given at an age when most stars choose quiet retirement.

In 1976, John Wayne was voted Star of the Year by the Hollywood Women's Press Club. Seen with him were his old friends Shirley Temple Black and Glenn Ford.

Duke felt a deep responsibility to Hollywood and "the industry." He could be counted on to show up at events like the 18th annual SHARE Benefit where he was greeted warmly by Steve McQueen.

because of its simplicity. In its favorite settings of war and the old West, issues were always clear cut, right and wrong, clearly demarcated. Wayne stood for a time when self-reliance was the great ideal, when honor, integrity, generosity and love of country were prized. Wayne remained a hero in an age of anti-heroes. That, in itself, was an accomplishment of huge dimensions.

Duke returned to Arizona for *Chisum* (which won him a third Oscar nomination) directly after the Awards ceremony. He was greeted by the entire company, every member wearing eye patches.

Obviously the character of *Rooster Cogburn* deserved a sequel and writer Martin Julien was assigned the tricky job of contriving a story that would continue the adventures of the one-eyed, hard-drinking, hair-trigger U.S. marshal. Inevitably the author turned to the time-honored device of putting Rooster into a position of conflict with a woman, Miss Eula Goodnight, a direct opposite in character, a holy roller whose mission has been decimated by a vicious young killer. The infuriated Bible-thumper sets out to avenge the dastardly deed. Armed with a carbine—and her Bible—she joins the U.S. Cavalry

Duke with Angie Dickensor. and her daughter Nikki, at the 37th annual Golden Apple Awards held at the Beverly Wilshire Hotel in 1977.

and, to his horror, travels beside Rooster Cogburn, who has been drawn out of retirement to pursue the "bad man."

As the original novel was written for John Wayne, the character of Miss Goodnight began to read more and more like Katharine Hepburn as each page of the treatment and script came out of the author's typewriter.

Would Hepburn play it? Of course she would and the event was important enough for national television cameras to go to the studio on the first day of shooting and interview the two legendary stars.

Asked why she had not appeared with Wayne before, Katie answered directly, "He never asked me."

The review of *Rooster Cogburn* in *Time Magazine* said it all:

"Wayne and Hepburn have outlived the cleverness and malice of critics and commentators. They have accumulated such tremendous energy of personality and survival that they outface such shattering pygmies by their mere presence. This presence is not so 'mere'—it is also our presence. There is something exhilarating and disturbing about watching the great long-lived movie stars in their last films,

John and Pilar Wayne, attending the American Film Industry dinner honoring Duke's close friend, "surrogate father" and the man who directed many of his biggest hits, John Ford.

perhaps even more so today when we are strangely out of touch with older people . . . So it is almost pointless to complain that *Rooster Cogburn* doesn't do justice to its stars. Almost, but not quite. The only reason to see this movie is to witness this gentle collision of two larger-than-life people who have spent their lives as professional incarnations of our fantasies, and who have earned the right to be incarnations of themselves."

After *True Grit,* Wayne pictures were not the sure-fire draws they once were, which didn't exactly warrant classifying them as failures. There was such a thing as a "Wayne gross" and both producers and exhibitors knew it so long they took it for granted. In 1975 Wayne dropped out of the first ten in the exhibitors' poll for the first time since he began heading it.

The Wayne compound was at Newport by the sea. The Duke lived in a large, cheery house and there were celebrations throughout the year when all the children assembled with their wives, husbands and grandchildren. These, for Duke, who had so little time for his family when he was younger, were moments of great joy in his last years.

Pilar lived in a house nearby. They spoke to each other daily on the telephone. The couple separated in 1973, and various reasons were advanced for the breakup. "Other women" of course were blamed. Then, they said Pilar got weary of all the demands made on her—that being a movie wife suited a certain period of her life—but it had become inconsistent with Duke's age and his health. She wanted him to settle down. She fought the long hard battle that led him to quit cigarette smoking. And there was more—much more—that Pilar could take credit for.

Among the Wayne wives, Pilar gave the appearance of having been the jackpot, the tough one, determined to survive. Besides being pretty, she was bright and intelligent. She was able to influence Duke. She quieted him down when that fabled temper flared. She once said, "Maybe we were destined to live apart and yet remain in love."

I once wrote, more than a decade before he died, that age was his only enemy—that to count him out was premature—that Wayne would never buy retirement or any cancellation of the morning "call" sheet until he had done his best to cheat the guy with the scythe—and perhaps, to enjoy a few more snarls at the Eastern establishment.

I wrote:

"For all hands, East and West, that would be a good thing. Better a snarling, battling curmudgeon like Wayne to have lived with, gotten angry with —and enjoyed—than one of those actors they end up describing as a man who never did anything wrong.

"Duke's right when he says he's lasted so long as a popular actor because he was lucky in getting good directors, and stories that had something. No one ever went out of the theatre disappointed.

"As Duke says, 'It was all right to pay twenty-five cents, wasn't it? Remember?' "

"Chisum," like True Grit, came late in Wayne's career and won him an Oscar nomination. Forrest Tucker is his adversary in this typical action scene.

The Films of John Wayne

Stagecoach was released on February 15, 1939. While it was the picture which finally established John Wayne as a major screen actor, it was actually the 65th film in which he had appeared!

His early film work, which began with an "extra" appearance in *Mother Machree,* 1928, can be divided into four categories. His first film appearances were bit parts at Fox and Warners. These were followed by second leads, usually played on loan-out from Columbia, his home studio. During his days on Poverty Row, he appeared in serials and for Lone Trail Productions as "Singin' Sandy" in five-reel Westerns. Finally, under contract to Republic Pictures, he did several pictures in the *Three Mesquiteer* and *Stoney Brooke* series.

Following is a complete listing of John Wayne's films starting with *Stagecoach,* the film that made him.

1939

STAGECOACH; co-stars: Claire Trevor, Thomas Mitchell, John Carradine, Andy Devine; director: John Ford.

THE NIGHT RIDERS; co-stars: Ray Corrigan, Max Terhune; director: George Sherman.

THREE TEXAS STEERS; co-star: Carole Landis; director: George Sherman.

WYOMING OUTLAW; co-stars: Adele Pearce, Ray Corrigan; director: George Sherman.

NEW FRONTIER; co-star: Phyllis Isley (Jennifer Jones); director: George Sherman.

ALLEGHENY UPRISING; co-stars: Claire Trevor, George Sanders, Brian Donlevy; director: William Seiter.

1940

DARK COMMAND; co-stars: Claire Trevor, Walter Pidgeon; director: Raoul Walsh.

THREE FACES WEST; co-stars: Sigrid Gurie, Charles Coburn; director: Bernard Vorhaus.

THE LONG VOYAGE HOME; co-stars: Thomas Mitchell, Barry Fitzgerald, Ward Bond, Mildred Natwick; director: John Ford.

SEVEN SINNERS; co-star: Marlene Dietrich; director: Tay Garnett.

1941

A MAN BETRAYED; co-stars: Frances Dee, Edward Ellis, Ward Bond; director: John H. Auer.

LADY FROM LOUISIANA; co-star: Ona Munson; director: Bernard Vorhaus.

THE SHEPHERD OF THE HILLS; co-stars: Betty Field, Harry Carey, James Barton, Ward Bond; director: Henry Hathaway.

LADY FOR A NIGHT; co-star: Joan Blondell; director: Leigh Jason.

1942

REAP THE WILD WIND; co-stars: Ray Milland, Paulette Goddard, Raymond Massey, Robert Preston, Susan Hayward; director: Cecil B. DeMille.

THE SPOILERS; co-stars: Marlene Dietrich, Randolph Scott, Margaret Lindsay, Harry Carey, Richard Barthelmess, William Farnum, George Cleveland; director: Ray Enright.

IN OLD CALIFORNIA; co-stars: Binnie Barnes, Patsy Kelly, Edgar Kennedy; director: William McGann.

FLYING TIGERS; co-stars: Anna Lee, Mae Clarke; director: David Miller.

REUNION IN FRANCE; co-stars: Joan Crawford, Philip Dorn, John Carradine; director: Jules Dassin.

PITTSBURGH; co-stars: Marlene Dietrich, Randolph Scott; director: Lewis Seiler.

1943

A LADY TAKES A CHANCE; co-stars: Jean Arthur, Charles Winninger, Grant Withers; director: William A. Seiter.

IN OLD OKLAHOMA; co-stars: Martha Scott, George "Gabby" Hayes, Grant Withers, Marjorie Rambeau; director: Albert S. Rogell.

1944

THE FIGHTING SEABEES; co-stars: Susan Hayward, Dennis O'Keefe, William Frawley, Grant Withers; director: Howard Lydecker and Edward Ludwig.

TALL IN THE SADDLE; co-stars: Ella Raines, Ward Bond, George "Gabby" Hayes; director: Edwin L. Marin.

1945

FLAME OF THE BARBARY COAST; co-stars: Ann Dvorak, Joseph Schildkraut, William Frawley; director: Joseph Kane.

BACK TO BATAAN; co-star: Anthony Quinn; director: Edward Dmytryk.

DAKOTA; co-stars: Vera Hruba Ralston, Walter Brennan, Ward Bond, Ona Munson; director: Joseph Kane.

THEY WERE EXPENDABLE; co-stars: Robert Montgomery, Donna Reed, Jack Holt, Ward Bond; director: John Ford.

1946
WITHOUT RESERVATIONS; co-stars: Claudette Colbert, Don DeFore; director: Mervyn LeRoy.

1947
ANGEL AND THE BADMAN; co-stars: Gail Russell, Harry Carey, Bruce Cabot, Irene Rich, Tom Powers; director: James Edward Grant.
TYCOON; co-stars: Laraine Day, Sir Cedric Hardwicke, James Gleason, Anthony Quinn; director: Richard Wallace.

1948
FORT APACHE; co-stars: Henry Fonda, Shirley Temple, Ward Bond, Irene Rich, George O'Brien, Anna Lee, Victor McLaglen, Dick Foran; director: John Ford.
RED RIVER; co-stars: Montgomery Clift, Walter Brennan, Joanne Dru, Harry Carey, Sr., Harry Carey, Jr., John Ireland, Coleen Gray; director: Howard Hawks.
THREE GODFATHERS; co-stars: Pedro Armendariz, Harry Carey, Jr., Ward Bond, Mae Marsh; director: John Ford.
WAKE OF THE RED WITCH; co-stars: Gail Russell, Gig Young; director: Edward Ludwig.

1949
SHE WORE A YELLOW RIBBON; co-stars: Joanne Dru, Harry Carey, Jr., Victor McLaglen, Mildren Natwick, George O'Brien, Tom Tyler; director: John Ford.
THE FIGHTING KENTUCKIAN; co-stars: Vera Ralston, Oliver Hardy; director: George Waggner.
SANDS OF IWO JIMA; co-star: Forrest Tucker; director: Allan Dwan.

1950
RIO GRANDE; co-stars: Maureen O'Hara, J. Carrol Naish, Victor McLaglen, Chill Wills, Harry Carey, Jr., Grant Withers; director: John Ford.

1951
OPERATION PACIFIC; co-stars: Patricia Neal, Ward Bond; director: George Waggner.
FLYING LEATHERNECKS: co-stars: Robert Ryan, Don Taylor, Jay C. Flippen, James Bell; director: Nicholas Ray.

1952
THE QUIET MAN; co-stars: Maureen O'Hara, Barry Fitzgerald, Ward Bond, Victor McLaglen, Mildred Natwick; director: John Ford.
BIG JIM McLAIN; co-stars: Nancy Olson, James Arness; director: Edward Ludwig.

After Duke loped into the ranks of the top box office stars, a Wayne role was carefully tailored to his acting skill and public image. Above, with Lana Turner in "The Sea Chase." Right, in "The Circus World."

Duke hit virtually all the major studios at one time or another in his long career. For Paramount he made "The Sons of Katie Elder," costarring Dean Martin.

1953
TROUBLE ALONG THE WAY; co-stars: Donna Reed, Charles Coburn; director: Michael Curtiz.

ISLAND IN THE SKY; co-stars: Lloyd Nolan, James Arness, Andy Devine, Harry Carey, Jr.; director: William A. Wellman.

HONDO; co-stars: Geraldine Page, Ward Bond, James Arness; director: John Farrow.

1954
THE HIGH AND THE MIGHTY; co-stars: Claire Trevor, Laraine Day; director: William A. Wellman.

1955
THE SEA CHASE; co-stars: Lana Turner, James Arness; director: John Farrow.

BLOOD ALLEY; co-stars: Lauren Bacall, Mike Mazurki, Anita Ekberg; director: William A. Wellman.

1956
THE CONQUEROR; co-stars: Susan Hayward, Pedro Armendariz, Agnes Moorehead, Thomas Gomez; director: Dick Powell.

THE SEARCHERS; co-stars: Jeffrey Hunter, Vera Miles, Natalie Wood, Olive Carey; director: John Ford.

1957
THE WINGS OF EAGLES; co-stars: Dan Dailey, Maureen O'Hara, Ward Bond, Edmund Lowe; director: John Ford.

JET PILOT; co-stars: Janet Leigh, Jay C. Flippen; director: Josef von Sternberg.

LEGEND OF THE LOST; co-stars: Sophia Loren, Rossano Brazzi; director: Henry Hathaway.

1958
I MARRIED A WOMAN; co-stars: George Gobel, Diana Dors; director: Hal Kanter.

THE BARBARIAN AND THE GEISHA; co-stars: Eiko Ando, Sam Jaffe; director: John Huston.

1959
RIO BRAVO; co-stars: Dean Martin, Angie Dickinson, Walter Brennan, Ward Bond; director: Howard Hawks.

THE HORSE SOLDIERS; co-stars: William Holden, Constance Towers, Hoot Gibson; director: John Ford.

In "Cast A Giant Shadow," Wayne played the cameo role of General Randolph, Chief of Staff of American Forces in the Italian campaign. Kirk Douglas starred.

Rock Hudson was Wayne's costar in "The Undefeated," the drama of a Union and Confederate soldier who become involved in another Civil War—the Mexican Revolution.

"Rio Lobo" was Duke's first picture after winning the Academy Award. He played a cavalry officer in a rough and tumble action piece about carpetbaggers vs. settlers in Texas. Duke's leading lady was Jennifer O'Neill.

1960
***THE ALAMO; co-stars: Richard Widmark, Laurence Harvey, Frankie Avalon, Patrick Wayne, Linda Cristal, Chill Wills, Veda Ann Borg; director: John Wayne.
NORTH TO ALASKA; co-stars: Stewart Granger, Ernie Kovacs, Fabian, Capucine; director: Henry Hathaway.

1961
THE COMANCHEROS; co-stars: Stuart Whitman, Ina Balin, Lee Marvin, Bruce Cabot, Bob Steele; director: Michael Curtiz.

1962
THE MAN WHO SHOT LIBERTY VALANCE; co-stars: James Stewart, Vera Miles, Lee Marvin, Edmond O'Brien, Andy Devine; director: John Ford.
HATARI; co-stars: Elsa Martinelli, Bruce Cabot; director: Howard Hawks.
THE LONGEST DAY; Cameo role; directors: Ken Annakin, Andrew Martin and Bernhard Wicki.
HOW THE WEST WAS WON; Cameo role; directors: Henry Hathaway, John Ford and George Marshall.

1963
DONOVAN'S REEF; co-stars: Lee Marvin, Cesar Romero, Dorothy Lamour; director: John Ford.
McLINTOCK!; co-stars: Maureen O'Hara, Patrick Wayne, Yvonne De Carlo, Chill Wills, Bruce Cabot, Edgar Buchanan; director: Andrew V. McLaglen.

1964
CIRCUS WORLD; co-stars: Claudia Cardinale, Rita Hayworth, Lloyd Nolan; director: Henry Hathaway.

1965
THE GREATEST STORY EVER TOLD; Cameo role; director: George Stevens.
IN HARM'S WAY; co-stars: Kirk Douglas, Patricia Neal, Bruce Cabot, Dana Andrews; director: Otto Preminger.
THE SONS OF KATIE ELDER; co-stars: Dean Martin, Martha Hyer, George Kennedy; director: Henry Hathaway.

1966
CAST A GIANT SHADOW; Cameo role; director: Melville Shavelson.

1967
THE WAR WAGON; co-stars: Kirk Douglas, Howard Keel, Bruce Cabot; director: Burt Kennedy.
EL DORADO; co-stars: Robert Mitchum, James Caan, Edward Asner; director: Howard Hawks.

1968
THE GREEN BERETS; co-stars: David Janssen, Jim Hutton, Raymond St

JOHN WAYNE · KATHARINE HEPBURN

A HAL WALLIS Production

ROOSTER COGBURN (...and the Lady)

Co-starring RICHARD JORDAN · ANTHONY ZERBE · JOHN McINTIRE · PAUL KOSLO · RICHARD ROMANCITO · TOMMY LEE · STROTHER MARTIN
Written by MARTIN JULIEN · Suggested by the character "Rooster Cogburn" from the novel TRUE GRIT by CHARLES PORTIS · Directed by STUART MILLAR
Music by LAURENCE ROSENTHAL · Associate Producer PAUL NATHAN · Produced by HAL B. WALLIS
A UNIVERSAL PICTURE · TECHNICOLOR · PANAVISION

This is a poster for "Rooster Cogburn," a sequel to "True Grit." The teaming of Katharine Hepburn and the Duke was considered important enough for the announcement to be covered by television. Years earlier, Hepburn told friends she wanted to work with Wayne.

This is the poster of Duke's last film—"The Shootist" in which the grizzled old veteran costarred with another vintage star, Lauren Bacall, and faced his final shoot-out.

DINO DE LAURENTIIS presents
A FRANKOVICH/SELF Production

JOHN WAYNE
LAUREN BACALL

IN A SIEGEL FILM

"THE SHOOTIST"

Co-Starring RON HOWARD · Guest Stars JAMES STEWART · RICHARD BOONE · JOHN CARRADINE
SCATMAN CROTHERS · RICHARD LENZ · HARRY MORGAN · SHEREE NORTH · HUGH O'BRIAN
Music by ELMER BERNSTEIN · Screenplay by MILES HOOD SWARTHOUT and SCOTT HALE
Based on the novel by GLENDON SWARTHOUT · Produced by M. J. FRANKOVICH and WILLIAM SELF
Directed by DON SIEGEL · Technicolor · A Paramount Release

Jacques, Bruce Cabot; directors: John Wayne and Ray Kellogg.
HELLFIGHTERS; co-stars: Katherine Ross, Vera Miles, Jim Hutton, Jay C. Flippen, Bruce Cabot; director: Andrew V. McLaglen.

1969
**TRUE GRIT; co-stars: Glen Campbell, Kim Darby; director: Henry Hathaway.
THE UNDEFEATED; co-star: Rock Hudson; director: Andrew V. McLaglen.

1970
*CHISUM; co-stars: Forrest Tucker, Christopher George, Bruce Cabot; director: Andrew V. McLaglen.
RIO LOBO; co-star: Jennifer O'Neill; director: Howard Hawks.

1971
BIG JAKE; co-stars: Richard Boone, Maureen O'Hara, Patrick Wayne, Bruce Cabot; director: George Sherman.

1972
THE COWBOYS; co-stars: Roscoe Lee Browne, Bruce Dern, Colleen Dewhurst; director: Mark Rydell.

1973
THE TRAIN ROBBERS; co-stars: Ann-Margret, Ben Johnson, Ricardo Montalban; director: Burt Kennedy.
CAHILL; co-star: Marie Windsor; director: Andrew V. McLaglen.

1974
McQ; co-stars: Eddie Albert, Diana Muldaur, Julie Adams, Colleen Dewhurst; director: John Sturges.

1975
BRANNIGAN; co-stars: Richard Attenborough, Judy Geeson, Mel Ferrer; director: Douglas Hickox.
ROOSTER COGBURN; co-star: Katharine Hepburn; director: Stuart Miller.

1976
THE SHOOTIST; co-stars: Lauren Bacall, James Stewart, Richard Boone, John Carradine, Hugh O'Brian, Ron Howard; director: Don Siegel.

* Academy Award Nomination.
** Winner of the Academy Award.
*** Four Academy Award nominations for photography, music, supporting actor and best picture. None awarded.